101 Questions & Answers on the Mass

REVISED, UPDATED EDITION

Kevin W. Irwin

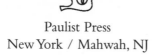

Paulist Press
New York / Mahwah, NJ

This is a revised, updated edition of *Responses to 101 Questions on the Mass* © 1999 by Kevin W. Irwin.

Scripture texts in this work are taken from the New American Bible, revised edition © 2010, 1991, 1986, 1970, Confraternity of Christian Doctrine, Washington, DC, and are used by permission of the copyright owner. All rights reserved. No part of the New American Bible may be reproduced in any form without permission in writing from the copyright owner.

Reprinted with permission: excerpts from the English translation of the Introduction to the *Lectionary for Mass* © 1969, 1981, 1997, International Commission on English in the Liturgy Corporation (ICEL); excerpts from the English translation of the Introduction to the *Rite of Baptism for Children* © 1969, ICEL; excerpts from the English translation of *Directory for Masses with Children* © 1973, ICEL; excerpts from the English translation of *Dedication of a Church and an Altar* © 1978, ICEL; excerpts from the English translation of *The Roman Missal* © 2010, ICEL. All rights reserved.

Excerpts from the *Code of Canons of the Eastern Churches: Latin-English Edition, New English Translation* copyright © 2001, Canon Law Society of America, Washington, DC, are reprinted with permission. All rights reserved.

Cover image courtesy of iStockphoto.com/FrankyDeMeyer
Cover design by Sharyn Banks
Book design by Lynn Else

ISBN 978-0-8091-4779-3
Library of Congress Control Number: 2012941065

Published by Paulist Press
997 Macarthur Boulevard
Mahwah, New Jersey 07430

www.paulistpress.com

Printed and bound in the
United States of America

To
Rev. Walter G. Lewis

Contents

III. *Reform of the Liturgy* (QUESTIONS 18–24)

IX. *Eucharistic Doctrine and Discipline* (QUESTIONS 90–97)

X. *The Eucharist and Daily Life* (QUESTIONS 98–101)

Introduction

Why This Revision?

There are two main reasons. The first is the publication of a number of official church documents and revised versions of previous documents having to do with the theology and liturgy of the Eucharist upon which this book is based. The second is the revised English-language translation of the Roman Missal and the fact that many of the responses here use the Missal's texts for support and verification.

Among the new documents are

- Pope John Paul II's encyclical *Ecclesia de Eucharistia* on the theology of the Eucharist and the relationship of the Eucharist to the church (2003)
- Pope John Paul II's apostolic letter *Spiritus et Sponsa* on the fortieth anniversary of the Constitution on the Sacred Liturgy of Vatican II (2003)
- Pope John Paul II's apostolic letter *Mane Nobiscum Domine,* which introduced the celebration of the Year of the Eucharist (2004)
- Pope Benedict XVI's post-synodal apostolic exhortations *Sacramentum Caritatis* on the Eucharist (2007) and *Verbum Domini* on the Word of God (2010)
- Pope Benedict XVI's apostolic letter (*motu proprio*) *Summorum Pontificum* on expanding permission to celebrate the Tridentine Mass (2007) and its accompanying *Letter* (2007)
- The instruction from the Pontifical Council Ecclesia Dei entitled *On the Application of the Apostolic Letter Summorum Pontificum* (2011)

- The instructions from the Congregation for Divine Worship entitled *Liturgiam Authenticam* on liturgical translations (2001) and *Redemptionis Sacramentum* on things to be observed and avoided in the celebration of the Eucharist (2004)
- The Introduction to the *Book of the Gospels* in various editions (1997–2000)
- The document from the United States Catholic Conference of Bishops (hereafter USCCB) entitled *Happy Are Those Who Are Called to His Supper: On Preparing to Receive Christ Worthily in the Eucharist* on proper preparation for and the disposition when receiving the Eucharist (2006)

Among the revised documents are

- The *General Instruction of the Roman Missal*, containing the Vatican protocols for celebrating Mass, with adaptations by the USCCB (Latin text, 2000 and 2002; interim English translation, 2002; final English translation, 2011)
- *Norms for the Distribution and Reception of Holy Communion Under Both Kinds in the Dioceses of the United States of America* (2002), replacing *This Holy and Living Sacrifice* (1975)
- *Built of Living Stones: Art, Architecture, and Worship*, containing guidelines of the (then-called) National Conference of Catholic Bishops (2000), which replaced *Environment and Art in Catholic Worship* (1978)
- *Sing to the Lord: Music in Divine Worship*, containing guidelines of the USCCB on music in the liturgy (2008), which is a revision of *Music in Catholic Worship* (1972)
- *Sunday Celebrations in the Absence of a Priest*, containing the ritual to be observed when no priest is available to celebrate Sunday Mass from the USCCB (2007), which replaced the first edition published in 1997

Among other sources are

- Vatican II's Constitution on the Sacred Liturgy, *Sacrosanctum Concilium* (1963)
- Various instructions and directives from diocesan bishops, often in the form of letters or memoranda issued by them directly or through the liturgy and worship offices of the dioceses

The Revised Translation of the Roman Missal —What We Pray Is What We Believe

There is an important principle that has been used since the fifth century that describes how we can explain the meaning of any part of liturgy. In summary form, it asserts that "the law of prayer is the law of belief." Originally it was asserted by Prosper of Aquitaine between 435 and 442, when he commented on the prayers that the church was then using as intercessions on Good Friday. (Perhaps you recall that in our present Good Friday liturgy, we use rather extended general intercessions: the intention is announced, silence follows, and then a prayer in the style of the Collect, the Prayer over the Gifts, and the Prayer after Communion concludes each of the ten parts to these intercessions.) Prosper commented on the style and structure of these prayers and stated that "the law of prayer establishes the law of belief." From that time to this (including explicit statements in the papal magisterium, for example, Pope Benedict XVI's post-synodal exhortation *Sacramentum Caritatis*), we have looked to what the liturgy says and does as a primary source for understanding what the liturgy is.

We will use this principle over and over in this book so that what we pray becomes a firm basis for what we believe. Because this is the case, we need to reflect on what the revised texts of the prayers of the Missal say and to respect that this new translation was done largely for the sake of greater accuracy. Hence, a second main reason why this book has been revised is to put it in harmony with the prayers of the Roman Missal.

How Do You Find the Answers to the 101 Questions?

That is **the** question, isn't it?

I recently gave a talk at a parish in Virginia on the revised translation of the Roman Missal. During the question period, a gentleman asked me where he could find the definitive answer to his (largely rubrical) questions about the Mass. I replied that his was a most astute question given our blogosphere culture in which many Web postings about the Catholic Church are from curious sources, many not at all official or authoritative that will use a phrase such as "a Vatican source says..."

There are a number of factors that go into determining the definitive answer. Allow me to offer two thoughts.

Relative Weight of Documents

Not all church documents carry the same theological or disciplinary "weight."

For example, it is always a good bet that a document from an ecumenical council, like the Liturgy Constitution from Vatican II, is the highest authoritative source we have. It is, literally, worth its weight in gold and deserves rereading and study. But it does not contain all the answers to the questions in this book or that you and I can ask about the Mass.

In effect, the first several paragraphs of the Constitution sketched out a thorough and compelling theology of the liturgy in general (nn. 1–20). It then went on to describe norms for the reform of the liturgy, again in general terms (nn. 21–46). Only then did it make assertions about the theology of the Eucharist specifically (nn. 47–49) and then offer some general norms on the reform of the liturgy of the Eucharist (nn. 50–58).

Therefore, as rich as this source is, you cannot use it to answer the kind of questions most of us have about the way the Mass is celebrated or the meaning of a particular part of the Mass.

It is for that reason that I listed the sixteen documents above, which are among the documents I used to research this revision. In addition, there are other church documents I will refer to throughout that I used in the previous edition of this book and that are still of great value. These are, for example, the canons of the (sixteenth-century) Council of Trent on the Eucharist and documents from other recent popes on the Eucharist, such as Pope Paul VI's encyclical *Mysterium Fidei* (1965).

But these documents do not contain the "final word" about the way the Mass is celebrated today. For that we need to review subsequent documents from the Vatican, from the United States Bishops' Conference, and from the diocesan bishops. For example, there are a number of instances in the *General Instruction on the Roman Missal* where decisions about posture and the location of the tabernacle (nn. 314–15) (among others) are left up to the local bishop.

When in Rome, Do as the Romans Do

This adage was coined before jet travel made it possible for greater numbers to travel to Rome itself. (I am thinking, for example, of the funeral for the late Pope John Paul II and his beatification in Rome.) But the phrase really means that we ought to observe what the local (diocesan) church does liturgically, with the presumption that they are conducting the liturgy correctly. So, when on vacation, business travel, or pilgrimage to special shrines and holy places, it is best to suspend judgment about the way the liturgy is celebrated if it is any different from what you are accustomed to. Sometimes differences in practices are because different local bishops have made different decisions.

Finger pointing—at people or at liturgical books—does not build up the Body of Christ. Respectful questioning and research through books like this one (and the sources on which it is based) can go a long way toward becoming informed about what are often slight differences in the way Mass is celebrated. Such an approach can help to foster the church unity and respect for others that ought to be a result of participating in the Mass.

An Attitude of Gratitude

I hope and pray that what is presented here will help all of us become more fully and deeply immersed in the celebration of the Eucharist—the very word means "thanksgiving." I am deeply grateful to all my past and present students at the Catholic University of America, to pastoral ministers in renewal programs and diocesan conferences whom I have met around the nation, and to priest-friends from the variety of my pastoral and teaching assignments, all of whom have shaped the way I approach the liturgy because of their questions and eagerness to do what is right liturgically and pastorally. As a priest-professor for thirty-five years, I can attest to the truth of the saying "By your pupils you'll be taught." Some of you will find your questions here (perhaps reframed or edited, but yours). Thank you for all of them and please keep them coming. Thank you, as well, for your pastoral care of the people of God, especially at a time of shrinking personnel and financial resources and often increased pastoral demands. Your pastoral ministry makes the church live and thrive. Your work makes the church work.

A final word of thanks to the priest-friend of over thirty years who has witnessed the evolution—not to say revision—of my knowledge of, thought about, and approach to the Eucharist. It is appropriate that the book I dedicate to him is a revision. One of the challenges of ongoing formation of clergy is that we not rest (only) on what we learned in seminary, but that we keep updated in the variety of fields that come to bear on pastoral ministry. Thanks to him and the countless priests like him "in the trenches" whose pastoral example encourages academics like me to continue to work through what we have learned, to teach, and to offer fresh and new insights from our tradition to ever-changing circumstances of church life. That is why a revision of a book like this is necessary. Thanks, too, to the editors of the Paulist Press for the invitation to put pen to paper again and to offer a revision of this book. They are Larry Boadt, CSP (RIP), Mark-David Janus, CSP, Don Brophy, and Donna Crilly.

I

Background and Terminology

1. Where does the term *Mass* come from? Is the Mass the same thing as the sacrament of the Eucharist?

Who am I to debate with Shakespeare that "a rose by any other name would smell as sweet"? But, in fact, your question about the names for this sacrament is very important because we use a number of terms to describe it and for a variety of reasons. The short answer is yes; the term *Mass* refers to the sacrament of the Eucharist where the mystery of our salvation is accomplished (from the Prayer over the Gifts, Holy Thursday Evening Mass).

Now the term *Mass* itself comes from the Latin text for the Dismissal—*Ite, missa est*—where the word *missio* means "sending forth." It literally connotes our being sent forth when the Eucharist has ended to live what we have celebrated. The translation in the Missal is "Go forth, the Mass is ended." After the Council of Trent (the church council that met in the sixteenth century to counteract the Reformation), Catholics used the term *Mass* to underscore that, central to our faith, was the celebration of the Eucharist and our belief in the real presence of Christ in the Eucharist, and that at the Eucharist we experience the same sacrifice that Christ endured for our salvation. This was to distinguish us from the Reformers and the subsequent Reformation churches, which emphasized the proclamation of the Word to such an extent that they did not emphasize the Liturgy of the Lord's Supper and the consecration of bread and wine as the enactment of Christ's sacrifice in this sacrament. (This statement should not be taken as a sharp division between us today. In the past forty years, both Catholics and other Christian churches have engaged in the reform of the liturgy to the extent that many other Christian churches celebrate the full Eucharist weekly, and we Catholics have grown in our appreciation of the proclamation of the Word at Mass.)

That Catholics still use the term *Mass* is clear from the Constitution on the Sacred Liturgy of Vatican II, which refers to the

Mass (n. 56) as containing both the Liturgy of the Word and the Liturgy of the Eucharist. This text is found in several post–Vatican II documents to underscore that today we Catholics want to stress that the Mass is the celebration of *both* the Word and the Eucharist. But sometimes today the term *Mass* is not used in favor of the expression *the celebration of the Eucharist* or *the liturgy*. The reason for this is to draw out the reality that the action of celebrating the Eucharist with the people's participation is central to what occurs. It is also helpful to remind ourselves that in Roman Catholicism we use the term *liturgy* to refer to all seven sacraments as well as other ritual actions of the church, including the Liturgy of the Hours, the dedication of churches, and more. This means that for us the term *liturgy* is much wider than the Eucharist or Mass.

Until recently it was common to refer to the celebration of the Eucharist at a wedding as a *Nuptial Mass*, from the Latin *nuptiae*, meaning "wedding." More commonly today we would use a phrase such as the *Wedding Eucharist*. Also it had been customary to use the term *dry Mass* to refer to a demonstration of the Mass for instructional purposes. Where this is done today, it is more accurately called a "dramatization" of the Mass lest it appear in any way to simulate the actual Mass. However, where you find the term *Mass* commonly used today is as a *healing Mass* or a *children's Mass*. But, in fact, every celebration of the Mass contains aspects of healing and so the phrase *healing Mass* is technically redundant. The term can be pastorally helpful, however, because people will know that the invocation of God's healing grace will be emphasized on these occasions for those physically ill or emotionally disturbed. Some people find these Masses very comforting as they deal with such human tragedies as terminal illness or sexual or emotional abuse. With regard to a children's Mass, the Vatican issued a special *Directory for Masses with Children* on the Solemnity of All Saints, November 1, 1973, which indicated that when there are a number of adults present, the children could be separated from the main assembly for the Liturgy of the Word (*Directory*, chapter 2), or that when there are many children and fewer adults present (chapter 3), some elements of the Mass could be accommodated to their age level and ability to participate.

There are also several other terms that describe the Eucharist; for example, the *Catechism of the Catholic Church* includes the *Lord's Supper*, the *breaking of bread*, the *memorial of the Lord's passion and resurrection*, the *holy sacrifice*, and *Holy Communion* (see nn. 1328–32), and each of these carries a connotation that points to one or another aspect of the Eucharist. Hence, to use the term the *Lord's Supper*, we are underscoring the meal aspect of the celebration. When we use the term *holy sacrifice*, we emphasize that through this action we experience the very same act of sacrifice Christ accomplished for our salvation.

In summary, I'd say that you will not find the term *Mass* used as much today as formerly but that it still has a place in our church vocabulary (hence the title for this book!). What you will more commonly find today is the term *Eucharist*, which emphasizes the Liturgy of the Eucharist and our active participation in both Word and Lord's Supper.

2. It sounds strange to use the word *celebrate* for such a formal ceremony. What are we supposed to be celebrating?

Your question is extremely important and at the heart of our faith life, which is clearly serious and profound. But it's also joyful and enriching of every aspect of our lives because our faith is in a God of the living who came that we might have life in abundance. The liturgy is formal in the sense that it's a ritual that we follow; we don't make it up as we go along. But in essence it's always about celebrating—experiencing again and again, more and more fully—the good news of our salvation in Christ and union with each other through him. Let me try to explain this more fully.

One prayer that commentators have used over the centuries (literally) to describe what we do at Mass is summarized in the sentence from the Prayer over the Gifts from Holy Thursday's Evening Mass of the Lord's Supper. I'm sure you know how important this

day is in our liturgical calendar—the beginning of the Easter
Triduum from Thursday night to Easter Sunday—and also that this
prayer is prayed over the gifts on the altar, soon to become the
body and blood of Christ, the mystery that is especially commemorated on this night. My point is that the placement of this text is
no accident and its importance cannot be overestimated. In this
prayer we pray that "whenever the memorial of this sacrifice is celebrated, the work of our redemption is accomplished."

Let's unpack this phrase by phrase. First of all, the wording of
your question and this phrase are extremely important because
they both use the plural pronoun *our*. Every time we celebrate the
Mass, it is always a prayer that *we* pray, for all *our* needs. Even when
the priest prays by himself in the liturgy, we say that he prays "in
the name of the church" (*in nomine ecclesiae*). The Mass is not the
priest's prayer only; it is the prayer of the whole church, here and
now and those who have gone before us—"in communion with
those whose memory we venerate" (as we pray in the Roman
Canon). Second, the phrase "the memorial of this sacrifice" reflects
the central place of the Mass in the whole Christian life; it is
unique because through the Mass we experience again and again
the very same sacrifice Christ offered for us: his obedient life,
humiliation, suffering, death, resurrection, and ascension. We know
that this happened once for all in historical time. We also know that
what we do in the liturgy is to experience that same redemption
in particular ways here and now. Jesus' one sacrifice has been
offered once for all; every time we celebrate the Mass we are drawn
into that same sacrifice again and again.

Let's look at another part of the church's prayer to help
explain how the liturgy is both the same sacrifice of Christ and our
appropriation of it in our need. In the Sunday Preface IV we hear:

> For by his birth he brought renewal
>   to humanity's fallen state,
>   and by his suffering, canceled out our sins;
>   by his rising from the dead

he has opened the way to eternal life,
and by ascending to you, O Father,
he has unlocked the gates of heaven.

All that Christ accomplished for us is offered for us in its fullness, depth, and riches as celebrated and experienced in the Mass. Hence, the third important phrase of our Holy Thursday prayer is "the work of our redemption is accomplished." Notice it does not say it is "repeated," or that we do something in addition to what Jesus did. It is the very same sacrificial death and resurrection that we experience through the words, symbols, gestures, and actions of the Mass—and we experience this paschal mystery in our need for it and for redemption. Think about why we need "redemption": our sense of alienation from God and each other, the sins we have committed and the things we have chosen not to do in our selfishness, the hurts we nurture into grudges, our making idols out of human accomplishments (perhaps even money) as opposed to our real identity and value from God's life and love within us. Once we acknowledge our need for redemption, then the Mass becomes more and more important as the principal way we experience redemption in our lives.

3. Why are Catholics obliged to attend Sunday Mass? It makes Mass seem like an unpleasant duty instead of a joyous celebration.

In answering the previous question, I emphasized how through the Mass we experience Christ's paschal mystery in a privileged and direct way—and that it is both solemn and joyful. Now this mystery is the heart of our faith. The acclamation after the Institution Narrative in the Eucharistic Prayer (previously called the Memorial Acclamation) is now called by the phrase that introduces it: the *Mystery of Faith*. The mystery of our faith, the heart of the matter, is the paschal mystery—Christ's death and resurrection, and our dying to sin and rising to real life through him. Because it is the key to all that we believe and because through the Mass we just don't think about it but we truly experience it and participate in it (literally "take part in it"), it makes sense that the church would want to insist on how important it is by making it obligatory. Put a different way: because it is so important, why wouldn't we want to go at least every Sunday?

Let me move to another level of your question: namely, why *Sunday* Mass is so important as opposed to other days of the week. Part of the answer comes from the Jewish origins of what we celebrate liturgically. In accord with the prescriptions of the Mosaic Law, Jews were to "keep holy the Sabbath day"—Saturday for us. This was the seventh day of creation, the day God rested and the day Jews were to remember their passing over from slavery to freedom through the Red Sea. Now if "the seventh day" was so important as the celebration of the covenant God made with the followers of Moses, it makes literal and symbolic sense that the early Christians adopted the next day—the eighth day—as the day when we would celebrate our relationship to God through the new covenant in Christ. But what we also celebrate at Sunday Mass is the breaking in of the new kingdom of God through Christ, what we technically call the eschatological "day of the Lord," the future kingdom in eternity. So Sunday becomes not only a day to look back at what Christ did once in history, but also a day to look forward to the time when there will be no more need for liturgy (or "when sacraments shall cease," as we sing in the familiar hymn), and we will participate in the banquet of the Lamb in the kingdom forever. Hence, it is quite logical and appropriate that *Sunday* Mass is regarded as qualitatively and theologically more important than the Eucharist we celebrate on any other day. It is the sacrament that makes the church as the church journeys to the kingdom of God.

Now I am well aware that there are places where, because of the shortage of ordained priests to serve as pastors, some parishes cannot offer Mass on every Sunday. When this happens, the people use a rather new form of Sunday liturgy entitled *Sunday Worship in the Absence of a Priest*. I'll say more about this later on (especially as I reply to questions number 5 and 6 specifically about this rite), but if you read the *General Instruction of the Roman Missal* and what the Vatican and the U.S. bishops have to say about the situation of "priestless parishes," what is clear is that because of the nature of Sunday as the key, pivotal day of the liturgical week, congregations should come together on the Lord's day, even "in the absence of a priest," to deepen its experience of Christ's paschal mystery, even though they cannot always celebrate the Eucharist in its fullness on Sunday.

Time was, of course, that the "Sunday obligation" meant Sunday from midnight to midnight and there was no such thing as the Saturday evening Mass. The rationale for permitting Sunday Mass to be celebrated on Saturday evening as well (the parallel is for the obligation of days of precept, otherwise called "holy days," to be satisfied the evening before these feasts) goes back to Judaism and the way it "tells time." From the Book of Genesis on, the Jews end and begin the day at sunset: as the Book of Genesis says of the days of creation, "evening came, and morning followed—the first day" (Gen 1:5). This was the religious and liturgical background for Christians to celebrate the start of Sunday at Saturday night Evening Prayer (part of the Liturgy of the Hours), as well as through all the other parts of the Hours and the Eucharist on Sunday. In effect, the liturgical time of any Sunday was always approximately thirty or so hours, not twenty-four, with the Eucharist as its high point. This precedent and the pastoral need of people who could not get to Sunday Mass led to the pastoral judgment to allow Masses on Saturday evenings to be Masses of Sunday for convenience. The intended "audience" for this accommodation were people who, for example, worked irregular hours or lived in places where a priest was available only on Saturday evenings because of Sunday commitments elsewhere. The intention behind the Saturday exception was that it not diminish the theology of Sunday and that it not be frequented regularly. At the same time, however, I think a certain pastoral judgment should both uphold the value of Sunday and appreciate that Saturday evening Masses can be especially convenient for the elderly who choose to go reg-

ularly on Saturdays because by that time of day their limbs coop-
erate and they can walk and get around easily, or they can avoid the
crush and rush of the Sunday morning parking-lot issues, or
because they know they feel "up to it" on Saturday but are not
always sure they will feel so well the next day. Lest they then miss
Mass on Sunday because they are moving slowly or don't feel well,
they legitimately choose to go on Saturday to avoid guilt. You'll
notice I said *guilt*. Clearly Sunday obligation does not oblige one
who is ill or infirm from age. They would not be guilty of sin for
not having participated in Sunday Mass. For the rest of us, however, it is a matter of grave obligation—and of privilege. (For more
on the theology of the Lord's day, read the apostolic letter of Pope
John Paul II, *Dies Domini*, issued in 1998.)

4. If the Mass is the prayer of those who come together, how come it is sometimes offered for special intentions or for people who aren't present?

Every Mass is for all the living and all the dead, or what we
call the communion of the saints. Phrases such as the one I mentioned in answer to question 2, "in communion with those whose
memory we venerate" (Roman Canon), and prayers such as—

> Lord, remember now
> all for whom we offer this sacrifice:
> especially your servant N. our Pope,
> N. our Bishop, and the whole Order of Bishops.
> all the clergy,
> those who take part in this offering,
> those gathered here before you,
> your entire people,
> and all who seek you with a sincere heart.
>
> (Eucharistic Prayer IV)

—remind us of this truth. The very term *Prayer of the Faithful* (otherwise called the Universal Prayer or the "bidding prayers") underscores this when (normally) the last two petitions are for the sick and the dead. It's at that point in the liturgy that we call to mind and heart those who are dear to us who cannot be present because of illness, old age, and so on.

The other place in the liturgy when the priest (silently) acknowledges those whom he would remember in a special way through the intercession of the Mass is during the pause after "let us pray" at the Collect (the opening prayer). Sometimes that is called the "Mass intention." Sometimes a priest may state this at the beginning of the Mass. Strictly speaking, there is no requirement that he do this. In some parishes, that person or need is named in the Prayer of the Faithful, which I judge to be its more proper place. This tradition of naming persons or needs goes far back in our church and is one way of expressing how the Mass is always for those who gather and for the whole church. If we belong to the communion of the saints, it makes sense to intercede for all the church at every Mass.

5. I live in a rural parish and when our priest cannot come for Mass we have a "Communion service" led by our deacon. I know this isn't a Mass. But could you tell me what it is?

Depending on your diocese, it may be that a number of parishes are experiencing the same thing you describe. This is because the number of ordained priests has declined but the demand for the Eucharist among the faithful has not. One of the strengths of American Catholicism was the evolution that took place from the early years of our being settled to the breadth and expanse of populating and settling across the U.S. territory. While it was not always the case that priests were available for Masses in the earlier decades of our nation's founding, eventually it became common for priests to be available for Sunday Mass in almost every part of our country. This was and is obviously not true for many other parts of the worldwide Catholic Church. In order to provide for the spiritual welfare of communities that cannot have Sunday Mass every week, the Vatican issued directives in 1988 about what such a priestless service should look like. This document specified that the community should gather on Sunday for a celebration of the Word of God and "also…when possible, by eucharistic communion." Note that the emphasis is on gathering for the Word; Communion is separate and sometimes it is not distributed. Hence, the term *Communion service* is really not totally accurate.

What your deacon is using is a ritual from a book prepared for the United States entitled *Sunday Worship in the Absence of a Priest*. In fact, this book contains two kinds of rituals. One is the "Celebration of Morning or Evening Prayer (with Holy Communion)." The other is the "Celebration of the Word of God (with Holy Communion)." From what you describe, the deacon probably used the latter structure and the scripture readings for that Sunday.

You are quite right that this ceremony is not the same as the Mass, even though it has many parallels. Unfortunately, it's not the same thing as the Mass where we present bread and wine at the Presentation of the Gifts, consecrate them during the Eucharistic Prayer, break the bread at the Lamb of God, and distribute it during Communion. In fact, in his encyclical *Ecclesia de Eucharistia*, Pope John Paul II spoke about "the sacramental incompleteness of these celebrations" (n. 32) because they are not the same thing as the celebration of the Mass, despite the fact that Communion may be distributed. As far back as 1742, Pope Benedict XIV stated that the priest and people should share in the same offering at Mass and that Communion should be given from hosts consecrated at that Mass. This principle has been repeated ever since, so that it is always preferential to receive Communion at the Mass during which the bread and wine were consecrated. When this doesn't happen, there is a lack of integrity in what we do—the act of offering Mass is separated from the act of receiving Communion. In other words, what this does is to separate what is inseparable. This is the same problem with these services without a priest. It's not a Mass where we take part in the offering of the Mass and receive Communion at the same action. It separates what should not be separated.

Sunday Worship in the Absence of a Priest is the best the church can offer until such time as there will be priests available for Mass every Sunday in every parish. For more background, why not read the introduction at the beginning of that ritual book? It's a very clear description of what this is and what it is not.

6. How did the rituals in the book *Sunday Celebrations in the Absence of a Priest* come about?

This is an example of the relationship of a national conference of bishops to Rome and vice versa. Soon after the 1988 Vatican document addressing this situation, the American bishops appointed a committee to discuss what such a ritual might look like and what it should contain. This resulted in the promulgation in 1993 of this ritual with an important "Introduction" addressing the theology of Sunday, the importance of Sunday Eucharist, and what this ritual is and is not. After some years of use, the bishops decided to revisit this ritual book and formed a task force to study it and suggest changes. This group submitted its recommendations to the USCCB Committee on the Liturgy (as it was then called), who in turn presented it to the bishops for approval. The ritual was subsequently sent to Rome for final approval. The present edition of *Sunday Celebrations in the Absence of a Priest* is a result of this confluence of the relationship of a national hierarchy with Rome and vice versa. Put differently, this is a unique example of a ritual that had its origins and evolution here in the United States. It is not a translation or reordering of a Roman ritual book.

The Canadian Catholic Conference issued its own ritual in 1995, *Sunday Celebration of the Word and Hours*.

In both cases, the ritual need not be led by a deacon, but if a deacon is present he is to lead the service.

7. Can you explain why our parish now celebrates baptisms at Sunday Mass? Does this change the meaning of the Mass?

Allow me to begin by talking a bit about the baptism of children itself as this frames the past and present practices of the way baptisms occur. The prevailing understanding of baptism before Vatican II was that by the pouring of water and the proclamation of the baptismal formula, the stain of original sin was removed and those baptized could now inherit the kingdom of heaven. Hence, one was to be baptized as soon as possible after birth.

There is nothing really wrong with this theology and it has not been overturned with the new rite for infant baptism after Vatican II. But what has occurred in the revision is the important restoration of a host of other images and meanings about baptism that are reflected in the new rite—among which is the theology that through baptism we become members of the church. In fact this "ecclesial consciousness," meaning our awareness of being members of each other in God's household, is an important emphasis in all our revised sacramental rituals since Vatican II. (For example, what was once only called "confession" is now called the Rite of Penance and of Reconciliation, meaning reconciliation with God and one another.) Belonging to the church as an essential part of the theology of the Eucharist runs through Pope John Paul II's encyclical *Ecclesia de Eucharistia*. That baptism leads to church membership is clear. That's why the Rite for the Baptism of Infants is now placed in the ritual for Christian initiation, with the understanding that baptism leads us to the central sacrament of our faith—the Eucharist. We are baptized, and through this sacrament of initiation we are made members of the church whose unique identity is celebrated and confirmed in the celebration of Mass. Therefore, there has always been a clear relationship between baptism and the Eucharist—which has been restored as a chief element of the present rite for infant baptism.

This is why many parishes celebrate baptisms at Sunday Mass. The *General Instruction* for the baptism of infants states:

> To bring out the paschal character of baptism, it is recommended that the sacrament be celebrated during the Easter Vigil or on Sunday, when the Church commemorates the Lord's resurrection. On Sunday, baptism may be celebrated even during Mass, so that the relationship between baptism and eucharist may be clearly seen; but this should not be done too often. (n. 9)

My judgment about that last phrase, "not done too often," reflects the church's wisdom that the communal celebration of each sacrament should stand on its own as just that—communal celebrations of the church's full liturgical life—and that other sacraments or rites should not always be added to the Mass (for example, Evening Prayer, baptisms, and so on). But when baptisms do occur at Mass, the relationship of belonging to the church and appreciating the Eucharist as a sacrament of initiation is made clear, and this is quite appropriate theologically and liturgically.

The frequency of when this occurs varies, depending on numbers and the parish preparation program. In any event, the theology behind this is ecclesial ("church") belonging and welcoming. One way that each of us can ratify this theology would be to be sure to participate in the Sunday Eucharist when baptisms occur when we can, and then after Mass to meet and greet the parents who had infants baptized in order to make them feel welcomed into the parish and the church at large.

Finally, a brief comment about your last question: does this change the Mass? It does not. What the celebration of baptism does is to bring out what is always implied in the Mass—that baptism is to be understood as the sacrament of initiation into the church, which celebrates Mass as its center of church belonging and the worship of God.

II

Liturgical Roles

8. I have always referred to the priest as the celebrant. My friend calls him the presider. Is there a difference?

Your question reminds me of the very first question in this book about names for the Mass and how different names bring out different aspects of the same reality. You speak about your using the term *celebrant*. This is a relatively common term in our tradition used to describe the priest's role as leader and the one who acts in the liturgy "in the person of Christ" (*in persona Christi*). In the Middle Ages, for example, the priest's power to consecrate the bread and wine was so important that it diminished emphasis on other liturgical roles, even that of the congregation. But with the emphasis—stated repeatedly in the Liturgy Constitution of Vatican II and since then—that the assembly is to participate actively and knowingly in the liturgy, it is not surprising that some have questioned whether the term *celebrant* is adequate to describe the priest's role. In a real sense all the baptized "celebrate" the liturgy.

Your friend's use of the term *presider* has official sanction in the *General Instruction of the Roman Missal* when it uses the terms *presider, preside,* and *presiding* no fewer than fifteen times. For example, in number 31, it states that the priest exercises "his office of presiding over the gathered assembly," and in the next paragraph it states that "the nature of the 'presidential' parts requires that they be spoken in a loud and clear voice and that everyone listen to them attentively." From as early as the second century, St. Justin the Martyr referred to the one who presides at the liturgy to distinguish him from others, such as the reader or deacon. The fact that certain prayers of the liturgy are designated as *presidential* prayers follows that tradition. These specific presidential prayers are the Eucharistic Prayer, Opening Prayer, Prayer over the Gifts, and Prayer after Communion. The term *presider* refers to the priest's precise role at these parts of the Mass as speaking in the name of Christ and the

church but in such a way that these actions do not diminish the role
of the whole assembly in celebrating the liturgy.

At the same time the *General Instruction of the Roman Missal* sanctions your use of the term *celebrant*. It refers to the celebrant of the
Mass (priest or bishop) twice the number of times it uses a variation
of *preside*. (If you add the term *concelebrant*, that number grows significantly.) My sense is that when *preside* or a variation is used, the term is
meant to refer to the particular liturgical functions that the ordained
are to fulfill. When *celebrant* is used, it most often refers to the person
of the priest or bishop himself as he functions in the liturgy.

9. If we're all celebrants at Mass, doesn't that mean we're all priests in some way?

Well, yes. Our theological tradition has always insisted that at
baptism we are made sharers in the royal priesthood of Christ. This
is solidly based on such New Testament texts as 1 Peter 2:9–10:
"You are 'a chosen race, a royal priesthood, a holy nation, a people
of [God's] own, so that you may announce the praises' of him who
called you out of darkness into his wonderful light." This is echoed
in the Sunday Preface I in referring to us as a "chosen race, a royal
priesthood, a holy nation, a people for your own possession." In
addition the *General Instruction of the Roman Missal* refers to the
"royal priesthood of the faithful" (n. 5) and to the assembly's exercising their "baptismal priesthood" (n. 69) by participating in the
Universal Prayer (Prayer of the Faithful).

10. Why, then, do we need a priest at all?

Because our theological tradition has also emphasized the
difference between what God makes us through baptism and what
God makes us through ordination. These are not the same realities.
Ordination is based on baptism and derives from the theology of
being consecrated to God. But it draws out one specific dimension
of baptism and consecrates a priest to serve the holy people of God
at the altar, in other liturgy, in preaching, and as a public witness to

Christ, the servant of all. The very term *priest* emphasizes the role of the ordained in offering the sacrifice of the Mass for and with all of us. He is not alone but he bears unique responsibility for the Mass. Ordination places the priest in a particular relationship to the whole church for and with whom he acts in the Mass. It also places him in relation to all the other ordained in the church—bishop, other priests, and deacons—as sacramental representatives of Christ. Ordination also places the priest in direct relationship to all who have gone before us in succession to the apostles as a source of inspiration and a reminder that we always act liturgically in the name of the whole, wider church from the apostles down to us. Finally, our tradition insists that ordination carries a permanent and lasting character so that a priest is always to act in the name of Christ when he acts in the liturgy, while at the same time he always acts in the name of the whole church (*in persona ecclesiae*) as Christ's representative. Ordination is more than delegating a person for a function. It changes him in a way that is permanent and lasting— for the sake of the church.

11. Laypeople seem to be taking a bigger role in the Mass. Years ago we didn't have lay readers or eucharistic ministers. Is this because of the priest shortage?

No. As a matter of fact, as far back as Justin the Martyr (around AD 150 or so), we have evidence that readers and deacons functioned at Mass. Then in the early Middle Ages, when priests were sent all over Europe to evangelize and celebrate the liturgy, it became common for them to assume such roles as reader and deacon. This was more efficient and reasonable because the priest was sometimes the only baptized person present! But by the late Middle Ages and as endorsed by the Missal we received after the Council of Trent, the priest himself had to perform all the actions of all the ministers and say all the words of the Missal in a "low" Mass. In that Missal, a low Mass referred to a Mass with just one priest and a server (no other liturgical roles), with no music, and with no use of incense. Interestingly, however, at a solemn high Mass according to the Tridentine Rite, priests dressed as a deacon and a subdeacon and did the parts of the Mass that were proper to those roles (deacons proclaimed the gospel, subdeacons proclaimed the epistle, and both assisted at the altar). So in a sense we did have some differentiation of liturgical roles even in the Tridentine Mass (now called "the extraordinary form" of the Mass).

With Vatican II we restored liturgical roles to a number of persons—readers, acolytes, deacons, and others. Eucharistic ministers are a slightly different case. It is true that it was only after Vatican II that they began to serve at Mass, largely because of the increased numbers of persons receiving Communion. Their role also extends to what deacons did in the early church—bring Communion to those not able to be present at Sunday Mass. Now it is common for both deacons and eucharistic ministers to bring the Eucharist to the homebound, to share the day's scriptures with them, and to pray with them.

12. How are lectors and eucharistic ministers chosen? Are they supposed to be exemplary Catholics?

The first criterion is competence. Not everyone has the gift for reading in public or for assisting at Mass with decorum and reverence. These roles should engage people in the liturgy and should serve, not dominate, the Mass. Repeated instructions from the U.S. bishops about selecting such ministers also insist that they be good Catholics whose lives reflect the sacred duties they undertake. This does not mean that they act "holier than thou," but it does mean that people who live lives that are scandalous should not minister at Mass.

13. What special skills should eucharistic ministers have?

They should know the parts of the Mass—especially the Rites of Communion—so well that they can carry out their role in distributing the Eucharist with reverence and care for those they serve. They should be able to respond to the aging and the sick who cannot come up to receive by going to them. They should also be aware of the rest of the ministers of Communion at Mass and "fill in" where necessary. After distribution, they should help consume any consecrated wine that remains and should assist with reserving any consecrated bread that remains.

Eucharistic ministers who bring the Eucharist to the homebound should have the ability to make them feel cared for. They should also be able to share the proclamation of the Word with them and their families, discuss the scriptures with them, and lead them in prayer. Because of the issue I raised (in questions 5 and 6) about worship in the absence of a priest, sometimes eucharistic ministers might be among those designated to lead such services. In this case they should have special training in leading public prayer.

14. I understand that seminarians are officially "installed" as acolytes or servers and laypersons are not. Why not?

Let me separate the two parts to your question and explain what "being installed" means and then who may be installed. In the Middle Ages, one who was destined to be ordained a priest was ordained to what were then called "minor" and "major" orders. The minor orders were porter, lector, exorcist, and acolyte. The major orders were subdeacon, deacon, and priest. What happened to this neat configuration was that, in 1972, Pope Paul VI issued a directive (or *motu proprio*), the title of which is *Ministeria Quaedam,* that eliminated the terms *minor* and *major orders* and referred to the rite whereby one became an officially designated reader or acolyte as an "installation." The reason for this was to emphasize that these were liturgical ministries that could be undertaken by laypersons as well as seminarians and not ordinations reserved only for those seeking priestly ordination. The specific text of the directive states "ministries may be assigned to lay Christians; hence, they are no longer to be considered as reserved to candidates for the sacrament of orders" (n. III).

In this same document, however, Paul VI also asserts that "in accordance with the ancient tradition of the Church, institution to the ministries of reader and acolyte is reserved to men" (n. VII). Because the ministry of reader is commonly shared today by both men and women, it is very rare that any layman would be so installed because installation would not be possible for women. In addition, now that the Vatican has ruled that diocesan bishops in the United States may allow women to serve at Mass in their dioceses, it is most unusual to find that a man has been officially installed as an acolyte. The only clear and obvious exceptions to these practices are for those men in training for the priesthood and the permanent diaconate who are now "installed" as readers and acolytes. In effect, this means that for the most part only seminarians and those in formation for the permanent diaconate are installed to these ministries, despite the fact that Paul VI intended installations to include laymen.

There is another distinction that I'd like to mention here—between "ordinary" and "extraordinary" ministers of Communion. The ordinary ministers are bishops, priests, and deacons. Others, for example, instituted acolytes or laity, are designated as extraordinary.

15. Why do lay liturgical ministers wear special garb in some parishes while in other places they wear ordinary clothes?

Because it is not a common occurrence, I'm sure it surprised you the first time you saw a layperson ministering at Mass in special clothing. But there are historical precedents for this. For example, in the Tridentine Mass every person in the sanctuary wore special liturgical clothing. This meant that the ordained (bishop, priest, deacon, and subdeacon) dressed in a number of layers: amice (the square white cloth tied around the neck), alb (the white garment under the colored vestments), cincture (a rope-like belt tied around the waist), stole (a strip of colored cloth around the neck), and chasuble, dalmatic, or tunic (the colored garment over the whole body). It also meant that those who served at the altar wore a cassock (a black or red loose-fitting, ankle-length robe) and surplice (a hip-length white garment over the cassock), and that choir members sometimes wore garments similar to those worn by the servers.

In the present Mass, however, the roles of server, reader, eucharistic minister, and cantor are often assumed by people who are not ordained, yet in some parishes they wear the alb, which was the clergy's "undergarment." Why? The principal reason is the statement in the *General Instruction of the Roman Missal* that "the sacred garment common to ordained and instituted ministers of any rank is the alb" (n. 336). Originally the alb was what we today call the baptismal garment, the white robe that the newly baptized wore after their immersion in water (or having water poured on them). From the fourth century, this white garment was the external sign of baptismal dignity and belonging to the church. In the present rites for initiation, both adults and children are to wear white garments. This was the origin of the alb (from Latin for "white"), the garment one wore when ministering at the liturgy. This became the undergarment for the ordained whose outer garments drew more attention and were usually much more elaborately designed. The purpose of returning the alb to all liturgical ministers was to remind us that we wear special clothing for special events, that the liturgy is just such an event, and that what all liturgical ministers have in common is their baptismal dignity and responsibility.

Some parishes, however, choose not to have any ministers other than the priest and deacon wear special garb. Why? The thinking is that wearing special garb can "clericalize" us all and seems to recall how only the ordained or those destined for ordination (the pre–Vatican II notion of altar servers) could minister at the liturgy. The clear emphasis of Vatican II on how all the baptized are called to holiness, and that liturgical ministry derives from our common baptism, not just ordination, makes this an understandable pastoral judgment. The only difficulty with this practice is that the opposite reaction could occur, that is, to clericalize the ordained even more and set them apart from other liturgical ministers and the parish at large because they are the only ones wearing special clothes. I suppose the pastoral application here is that we should take seriously our ministry to each other at the liturgy and outside the liturgy, and that liturgical ministry never be seen as a special status or privilege, no matter what we wear. The real issue is how what we do liturgically resonates with daily life; hence, having the ordained and the baptized serve at the altar reminds us all of our common baptismal calling, ministry, and service of each other.

16. I've heard of parishes where women aren't allowed to be liturgical ministers. Why is that?

From as far back as we have documentary evidence in history, only men were permitted to function in liturgical roles because these roles were viewed as leading men to ordination as priests and priesthood is reserved for males. This was true across the board in the whole Catholic Church. However, after Vatican II (and returning to an older custom of the church), many decisions about liturgical practices are now given to the determination of the bishop of a given diocese. Therefore, when the Vatican recently made the determination that women could act as altar servers, it also stated that the decision to allow this had to come from the local bishop of the diocese. In the vast majority of American dioceses, it is now the custom for women to function as readers, eucharistic ministers, and most recently altar servers. In the one or two dioceses that restrict liturgical ministries to men, however, the bishops' explanations cite how liturgical ministry classically led to ordination to the priesthood, and that they see the practice of limiting liturgical ministering to men as a way to foster priestly vocations.

17. What is the role of the deacon at Mass?

The *General Instruction of the Roman Missal* gives the instructions for the deacon's role at Mass (nn. 94, 171–86). In the Introductory Rites, the deacon carries the *Book of the Gospels* and places it on the altar. If incense is used, he assists the priest at this point to incense the altar, he himself incenses the gospel book, and he helps the priest incense the altar at the Preparation of the Gifts. In the Liturgy of the Word, he proclaims the gospel and announces the intentions of the Universal Prayer (Prayer of the Faithful). Sometimes (given requisite preparation and permission) he may preach the homily. At the Presentation of the Gifts, he prepares the altar, hands the priest the paten with the bread to be consecrated, pours wine and a little water into the chalice, and gives it to the priest. At the Final Doxology at the end of the Eucharistic Prayer, he stands next to the priest holding the chalice until the people have concluded, "Amen." He invites the assembly to exchange the Sign of Peace, assists in the distribution of Communion, and takes the Communion vessels to the side table and purifies them (either during or after Mass). He makes any necessary announcements after the Prayer after Communion, and after the priest's blessing he dismisses the people using one of the forms, such as "Go forth, the Mass is ended."

Of all these functions at Mass, two are of special significance because they link the Eucharist with daily life. The reason why the deacon announces the intentions for the General Intercessions and makes the announcements at the end of Mass is that his ministry spans church building and marketplace, bridges sanctuary and home. In the early church and now with the restored diaconate, it is the deacon who knows who is ill, who is in need of charity and social ministry. It is also he who brings to the community's attention church or social concerns, again as a way to bridge participating in the liturgy and living the gospel.

III

Reform of the Liturgy

18. How can there be a "new" Mass? I thought nothing new could be introduced after the last apostle died.

Your question reflects a keen insight about the limitations of revelation and that, yes, with the death of the last eyewitness to what Jesus said and did, the mission of Christ's coming among us to save and redeem us was completed. But at the same time, when it comes to unpacking the meaning of what Jesus said and did, the church has the responsibility in every age to explain that revelation as completely as possible and also to explore new ways for that revelation to be understood, communicated, and taught. Hence, we can proudly say that we Catholics are not fundamentalists or literalists, but that what was revealed in Christ is continually experienced and expressed anew in every age.

When it comes to the Liturgy of the Mass, I want to say two things at the same time. First, it is true that from the earliest evidence we have to the present Roman Rite, the structure of the Mass has been the same. But second, there has always been a tradition of variety in some parts of the way the liturgy was celebrated. When you hear the term the *new Mass* this is a translation of the Latin term *Novus Ordo Missae*, the "new Order of the Mass," with the adjective *novus* meaning the rite of the Mass that replaced the rite from Trent—often called the Tridentine Mass. (I will comment more on this form of the Mass in responding to questions 19 to 22.)

Regarding structure, it is clear that in the time of Justin the Martyr (AD 150), the Mass was composed of the proclamation of the scriptures, the proclamation of the Eucharistic Prayer during which the gifts are transformed, and the act of taking Communion. Over the centuries, however, this same skeletal structure has been embellished in a number of ways and for a good many reasons. For example, once the Liturgy of the Eucharist moved from small, hidden places to the basilicas of the city of Rome, beginning in the

31

fourth century, the need arose for processions to be added to the proclamation of the scriptures and the action at the altar. This meant that what was added to the simple structure of Justin the Martyr's time were processions at the Entrance, the Presentation of the Gifts, and Communion, and that these ritual actions were accompanied by music. These musical compositions were originally parts of the psalms or other inspired texts, set to music for all to sing. The technical terms for these times for singing were the *Introit*, the Offertory, and the Communion processions. Unfortunately, very often from the Middle Ages on, these texts were either sung by a choir or recited by the priest to himself. They were rarely sung by the whole congregation. It was not a surprise, therefore, that in the 1940s in Europe the more popular form of participation was to sing hymns at these parts of the liturgy even though the priest still recited the Latin antiphons (that is, the texts originally set to music to accompany the processions at the *Introit*, Offertory, and Communion) to himself. (I will discuss antiphons a bit more fully in replying to questions 85 to 89 about music at Mass.)

An even clearer example of the way the same skeletal structure of the Mass was adapted to different circumstances was the fact that when the Tridentine Missal was established as the norm for the whole church from the sixteenth century onward, provision was also made for those religious communities and some dioceses that had their own "rites" of the Mass to keep their practices and not conform "jot and tittle" with the then-new Tridentine Mass. For example, before Vatican II, Dominican priests used their own rite for the Mass during which the priest placed the wine and water in the chalice at the beginning of the Mass, and said very short prayers at the foot of the altar and at the Offertory. Similarly, the archdiocese of Milan was allowed to keep its own Mass structure, which included an additional prayer of the priest at the Presentation of the Gifts. Today the element of the Eucharist that differs most from place to place and from religious community to religious community is the calendar of the saints commemorated at the liturgy. There are lists of Benedictine, Franciscan, Dominican, Carmelite, and Jesuit saints, for example, each honored in their communities and not by the whole universal church. In the same way, we American Catholics honor saints who have particular meaning for us but who are not necessarily honored in the rest of the world, such as St. Elizabeth Ann Seton (January 4) and St. John Neumann (January 5).

19. Before Vatican II, the Mass was quieter and more prayerful. Now I have a hard time concentrating on my prayer. Why did they change it?

Let me take the last part of your question first. When the bishops at Vatican II described the kind of revision they wanted for the Mass and all the other liturgical rites of the church, they repeatedly stressed that the revised liturgy was to serve the "full, conscious and active participation" that the liturgy by its nature requires. This phrase (or a variation on it) was used over a dozen times in the Liturgy Constitution. The simple reason was that they were reacting to the Tridentine liturgy, which was usually more quiet and which supported a lot of personal prayer. That's what you recall and obviously miss.

But the Tridentine Mass was not the only Mass that ever existed in the church's history. And like all other kinds of liturgy (taken literally from the Greek term *leiturgia,* meaning "public work of the people"), it is meant to be a public rite that all of us take part in and share in, not only with our minds and hearts, but also with our voices and our bodies. Much of what we do today by means of participation—singing, using gestures, changing postures—was actually done in the Tridentine Mass but by other people: the choir, servers, other ministers. What the reform of the Mass after Vatican II did was to restore these actions, postures, and gestures to us—the whole assembly gathered for worship. They were ours by tradition and right; now they have been restored for our use. But any act of liturgy should also have its times for personal prayer, its pauses and silences.

For example, built into the pattern of the present Mass are times when there should be silences for our personal, heartfelt prayer: at the introduction of the Mass, before the Collect, after each of the readings, after the homily, and after Communion. This is to allow another level and kind of participation: in silence as well as speaking and gesturing.

But these important external changes are not meant to change your attitude about your need for other times of quiet and prayer. Succinctly put: all liturgy is prayer, but not all prayer is liturgy. In fact, I'd say that in order for the Mass to have its deepest impact on us we will need time for other quiet prayer: to reflect on the scriptures and to encounter God in the deepest recesses of our hearts for intimate conversation. Nor should liturgy be viewed as not having moments of quiet prayer in its structure. I suppose the trick here is not to see the Tridentine Mass and today's Mass—the extraordinary form and the ordinary form—as opposites but to strive for "a delicate balance" (to use the title of Edward Albee's play) between vocal and gestural participation on the one hand and silent, quiet reflection at times during the liturgy and certainly outside the liturgy on the other.

20. Are Masses in Latin still allowed?

Yes. You will recall that in answer to question 18, I made a distinction between the present rite of Mass in Latin (called the *Novus Ordo Missae*, the "new Order of Mass") and the Tridentine Mass in Latin (also called the extraordinary form of the Mass). Regarding the celebration of the new Order of Mass or parts of it in Latin, there are repeated statements from Rome about its desirability, especially for the celebration of Mass when people from many countries and languages come together. The most recent assertion of this recommendation is in Pope Benedict XVI's apostolic exhortation *Sacramentum Caritatis* (n. 62). In addition, some bishops permit the celebration of a *Novus Ordo* Mass at their cathedrals as one of the Sunday Masses.

In addition, the issue of the Latin language frequently appears in descriptions of music to be used at Mass, lest some of the great treasures of music written for the Mass in Latin be lost. Also in some musical guidelines, support is given for singing some of the parts of the Mass in Latin as a sign of the church's universality throughout the world. (Again see *Sacramentum Caritatis*, nn. 61–62.)

Citing both the *General Instruction* (n. 12) and Vatican II's *Constitution on the Sacred Liturgy* (n. 54), the American bishops summarized the issue this way in their latest document on music in the liturgy, *Sing to the Lord*:

> The use of the vernacular is the norm for most liturgical celebrations in the dioceses of the United States "for the sake of a better comprehension of the mystery being celebrated" [citing the *General Instruction*, n. 12]. However, care should be taken to foster the role of Latin in the Liturgy, particularly in liturgical song. Pastors should ensure "that the faithful may also be able to say or to sing together in Latin those parts of the Ordinary of the Mass which pertain to them." They should be able to sing these parts of the Mass proper to them, at least according to the simpler melodies. (n. 61)

21. I read recently that the pope is allowing the use of the "old" Mass. Can you explain?

There was an evolution that led to Pope Benedict's most recent document on the Tridentine Mass. Let me try to summarize it in chronological order, indicating the theological issues involved.

In 1984, the Congregation for Divine Worship issued the document *Quattuor Abhinc Annos*, which addressed those people who after over a decade of the use of the reformed liturgy still felt themselves attached to the Tridentine Mass. The document stated that the diocesan bishop may allow those who make a specific request to celebrate the Mass according to the Roman Missal of 1962. The document also asserted that even though this permission was given that there still had to be "unequivocal, even public, evidence that the priest and people petitioning have no ties with those who impugn the lawfulness and doctrinal soundness of the Roman Missal promulgated in 1970 by Pope Paul VI." This was a reference to the followers of Archbishop Marcel Lefebvre in what was sometimes called the "Catholic Traditionalist Movement" or the Society of St. Pius X. The effect of this document was that some bishops oversaw the establishment of the regular celebration of the Tridentine Mass once on a given Sunday at a location or locations that he designated in order to provide pastoral care for those who were still attached to the former liturgy. For example, in the archdiocese of Washington, DC, there are three such centers.

Then in 1988, Pope John Paul II himself issued an apostolic letter (entitled *Ecclesia Dei*, which means "Church of God") reaffirming the permission to celebrate the Tridentine Mass in certain specified circumstances. He addressed the pastoral need for those attached to the former Missal. But then he specifically added the very significant category of allowing permission for this Mass "to facilitate ecclesial communion..." specifically "for those priests, seminarians, religious communities or individuals until now linked in various ways to the society founded by Archbishop Lefebvre." The specific catalyst for this permission was the fact that in that same year, 1988, Archbishop Lefebvre ordained four bishops to serve the Society of St. Pius X. That act of defiance to the authority of the pope caused the Vatican to issue a decree excommunicating the four bishops. Thus what was underlying the second reason why the pope gave permission for the Tridentine Mass was for the reconciliation of this movement. With this same document, the pope established a Roman commission also named Ecclesia Dei, "Church of God," which I take as an important sign that ecclesiology is far and away the major issue at stake in the celebration of the Tridentine Masses.

Pope Benedict XVI has been very concerned about this possible reconciliation and discussed the possibility of expanding the use of the Tridentine Mass with the members of the Roman Curia (December 2005) and then with the College of Cardinals (March

2006). In July 2007, the pope issued an apostolic letter entitled *Summorum Pontificum* in which he expanded the occasions when the Tridentine Mass could be celebrated: at Masses celebrated without the people (what we often call a "private" Mass), Masses in religious communities who may wish to celebrate this form with the permission of their major superiors, and Masses in parishes "where a group of the faithful attached to the previous liturgical traditions exists stably" (other translations state "a stable group"). These parishioners should make their request to the rector or pastor of the parish and, if unsuccessful, they may then approach the bishop to grant permission. What is interesting is that in this document the pope also states that diocesan bishops may give permission for the celebration of confirmation according to the former Roman Ritual, that clerics in holy orders may use the Roman Breviary published in 1962, and that bishops may erect "a personal parish" for celebrations of the liturgy according to the older form of the Roman Rite. For example, in the diocese of Richmond, Virginia, Bishop Walter Sullivan erected the parish of St. Joseph as the "Tridentine parish."

What is also very interesting is that in addition to *Summorum Pontificum*, the pope wrote an accompanying "letter" to his brother bishops addressing what he judged to be the unjustified fear that the increased permission for the Tridentine Mass might undermine the authority of the Second Vatican Council. He argued that he did not envision this and that, in the case of the followers of Archbishop Lefebvre, the pope has continued theological discussions with the hope that they might be reconciled to the Catholic Church—hence a reiteration of his defense of the documents and teachings of Vatican II against the followers of Archbishop Lefebvre who renounce some of Vatican II's teaching. The pope also addressed the fear that increased celebration of this Mass would cause undue divisions within parish communities. The pope judged this was unfounded since, in his estimation, the number requesting this form would be small and that they would need a certain degree of liturgical formation and knowledge of the Latin language. He also insisted that *Summorum Pontificum* took nothing away from the authority of the diocesan bishop.

My own sense is that this letter may have increased the opportunities for the celebration of the Tridentine Mass in some dioceses in the United States but that in fact these are comparatively very few. From my own travels throughout Europe, I do see that there are regular celebrations of the Tridentine Mass in some parishes and that such are seen to be part of the regular Sunday Mass schedule. It also does not surprise me that Pope Benedict XVI is following in line with his predecessor to be very concerned about the reconciliation of this dissident group. After all, as the recent popes have emphasized and as we pray in the third Eucharistic Prayer, one of the goals of the Eucharist is that we "may become one body, one spirit in Christ." Again, the title of the 1988 document and of the pontifical commission overseeing its implementation also underscores ecclesiology.

That these two documents from 2007 raised some questions and left some things unanswered was not surprising, and a number of diocesan bishops and national bishops' conferences asked the Ecclesia Dei Commission for further information and interpretation. Most recently this commission issued its own "Instruction" with further specifics about the present use of the Tridentine Mass (May 2011). One of the more notable assertions in this document is that ordinaries (bishops and major superiors of men) were asked to offer their clergy and seminarians training in the Tridentine Mass, "including the study of Latin." Recall that Pope Benedict XVI noted that those requesting (and presumably celebrating) the Tridentine Mass should have the requisite knowledge of Latin. As a university professor, I cannot but applaud such a directive given the amount of church literature in Latin. I often tell my students that to get the real flavor of St. Augustine or St. Thomas Aquinas or the official magisterium of the church, you really need to study (and savor!) the texts in Latin. But again, note that the recommendation is for "ordinaries" to do this if they so choose. Fairly soon after the publication of this document, Archbishop Vincent Nichols of Westminster in London issued a statement that the seminarians under his care would not receive training in this form of celebrating the Mass until after ordination since there was already so much that was required in the seminary curriculum.

22. Why does the pope use the terms the *ordinary form* and the *extraordinary form* of the Mass?

He used this distinction in the letter accompanying *Summorum Pontificum* in the section that addressed whether the possibility of expanding the use of the Tridentine Mass derogates the authority of Vatican II. He explained that the Missal first published by Pope Paul VI and subsequently by Pope John Paul II was the "ordinary form" (*forma ordinaria*) of the Eucharistic Liturgy and that the last version of the *Missale Romanum* prior to the Second Vatican Council published with the authority of Pope John XXIII would be called the "extraordinary form" (*forma extraordinaria*) of the Mass. My own sense is that the vast majority of Masses are celebrated according to the ordinary form and comparatively few are celebrated in the extraordinary form.

23. I have read about the "Tridentine Rite." Is this the same thing as the Tridentine Mass?

When there are adjectives that accompany the word *rite*, most often they mean the practices of a geographical group or a religious community. But I can imagine that immediately you are saying, "We use the Roman Rite but we are not in Rome!" Fair enough. Let me explain.

One of the privileges I have in teaching the liturgy is that I am able to expose my students to various liturgical rites from Eastern and Western churches. The evolution of these rites is a fascinating (though complex!) object of study. For example, in western Europe a number of liturgical practices were in use in places such as modern-day France, Germany, Spain, and the United Kingdom from the fifth century on. These are often called the "non-Roman Western rites"— Gallican, Mozarabic, the Stowe Missal, and others. At the same time, some liturgical practices that were in use in Rome were brought by bishops and missionaries over the Alps and spread to some places in Europe. While the basic structure of the liturgy in the West was the same, local practices were used as well as some Roman additions. This meant, for example, that Gallican practices (France) were joined to Roman practices, which eventually came back over the Alps to Rome. An example of the influence of the Gallican Rite on the Roman Rite is the procession of palms on Palm Sunday of the Passion of the Lord. This started in Gaul in the sixth century and only in the eleventh was it a required part of the Roman Rite. Underlying this interchange is the process called inculturation—where the liturgy is adapted based on differing cultures. So this is my first point about the term *rite*—it is based on geographical location.

My second point is that sometimes before the Council of Trent some religious orders or communities had versions of some parts of the Mass that were not exactly what the Roman Rite followed. An example is that the Dominican Rite contained a very brief prayer at the Offertory and none of the five Offertory prayers that were used in the Roman Rite at that point in the Mass—hence my reference to differences in religious–community liturgies being called a "rite."

Despite some usages that you may read today in the popular press that there is a Tridentine "rite," what this term refers to, in fact, is the Roman Rite as revised after the Council of Trent. This gave us the Roman Breviary revised in 1568 after Trent and the Roman Missal revised in 1570, but still called the Roman Rite.

One of the more interesting things I do in class is to compare and contrast other rites with the Roman Rite and also to compare and contrast the liturgy of the Roman Rite as celebrated at different historical periods. In effect, a comparison of the Roman Rite Mass after Trent and after Vatican II would look this way:

Extraordinary Form	**Ordinary Form**
Prayers at the foot of the altar	Greeting and Penitential Rite
Roman Canon and twelve prefaces	Ten eucharistic prayers and
Communion under one species	ninety-five prefaces
Prologue to John's Gospel and prayer	Both species permitted
to St. Michael before the Dismissal	Blessing and Dismissal only
Only clerics or "altar boys" minister	Lay liturgical ministry, both genders

24. In the old days, the priest always spoke the words from the Missal. Now some priests seem to go beyond the book and add their own words. Is this permissible?

One of the features of the present Mass is that it gives priests several opportunities to offer comments that are not printed in the Missal. For example, at the beginning of the Mass he (or the deacon or another minister) can choose to briefly introduce the liturgy in his own words. He can make a comment to introduce the scriptures, as well as to introduce the Preface and Eucharistic Prayer. He can make a comment prior to the Dismissal. These are all legitimate variations in the way the Mass can be celebrated.

In addition to this, there are several places in the Mass when he can choose from options given in the Roman Missal. These include the structure of the Penitential Rite itself (see question 30), the choice of the presidential prayers (Collect, Prayer over the Gifts, Prayer after Communion) on weekdays that have no special feast day or that is not a special season (like Advent, Christmas, Lent, or Easter), and the Dismissal (see questions 83 and 84). One of the distinguishing characteristics of the Roman Rite, as opposed to the liturgical traditions from the East, for example, is the variety of prefaces (they now number over ninety!) and eucharistic prayers themselves (they now number ten: nine in the official Roman books and one added by some bishops' conferences, such as the United States Conference entitled "For Various Needs and Occasions").

IV

Introductory Rites

25. I like being greeted when I come into church and I like saying hello to my friends, but in other churches people slip in quietly and don't talk. Is there an ideal way for people to gather for Mass?

I'd say that the ideal way to gather for Mass is to do both. Certainly in the Tridentine Mass there was an emphasis on silence and reverence before and during the Mass. But even then, there were ushers who greeted us, helped us to our pews, and facilitated the procession to Communion (not to mention taking up the collection!). Today many parishes have a group called "ministers of hospitality" who greet us and who facilitate seating, the procession with gifts, Communion, and so on. But certainly today there is also legitimate emphasis on what it means to come together as a community of faith for Mass and this includes greeting other people. The *General Instruction of the Roman Missal* (n. 46) states that the "purpose [of the Introductory Rites] is to ensure that the faithful, who come together as one, establish communion and dispose themselves properly to listen to the Word of God and to celebrate the Eucharist worthily."

On the basis of this statement I would say that greeting others before Mass is a way to solidify a sense of community and common purpose in our gathering to celebrate the Mass. At the same time I would also recommend that we use some time before Mass begins and then during the Introductory Rites to be silent and to deepen our awareness of what we are undertaking as a community of God's faithful. It is also important that if we greet others beforehand, this greeting should not disturb others who themselves want to be silent and to recollect themselves before Mass.

Sometimes the church building facilitates this since many have a "commons" or gathering area outside the church itself where this kind of meeting and greeting can take place.

26. The Entrance Procession seems to exalt the priest. Wouldn't it be better to have him sit somewhere in the church and walk up quietly to the altar to begin the Mass?

Part of my answer is historical and part is theological. First, when the Christian church was first allowed to celebrate liturgy publicly and was recognized as a legitimate religion in the Roman Empire (this is commonly associated with the Edict of Milan in 313), the numbers of Christians grew and the places needed for worship had to be larger. It was at this time that Christianity took over the Roman basilicas and made them houses for worship. These long, normally rectangular buildings required a series of processions: for the priest and ministers at the start of Mass, for the gifts being brought to the altar, for the people at Communion, and for the priest and ministers at the end of the liturgy. These processions were also accompanied by music and still are to this day: at the Entrance (formerly called the *Introit*), at the Presentation of the Gifts (sometimes called the Offertory), at Communion, and after the Dismissal. The functional purpose of the entrance procession is to have the ministers in place for Mass. But the theological reason for the entrance procession and the procession at the end of Mass (recessional) is to signify what all of us do when we celebrate Mass—we gather for worship and are sent forth from worship. We gather in order to disperse, in order to live what we have celebrated.

One thing that might help relieve the impression that the procession is only about the priest is to review the *General Instruction*'s suggested list of who should be in the procession and see to it that these people all participate in the procession with the priest: the thurifer (the person carrying the censer if incense is used), ministers with lighted candles, and an acolyte or other minister carrying the cross. They are followed by the deacon carrying the *Book of the Gospels* and then the priest himself (*General Instruction*, n. 120). Another thing to understand is why the ministers bow to the altar and the priest and deacon kiss it. The emphasis in the procession is on the altar, the enduring symbol of Christ, whose sacrificial death and resurrection will be commemorated on it once more. From the time of St. Ambrose (fifth century) onward, this act of kissing the altar was seen to emphasize the centrality of Christ in what we do liturgically and the symbolism of the altar as connoting the sacrificial aspect of the Mass.

27. In some parishes, the *Book of the Gospels* is carried in procession at the beginning the Mass. Why?

The short answer to your question is that the *Book of the Gospels* (not all the scripture readings, but I'll treat that below) is to be carried by the deacon or the reader. The better answer, however, is to explain what the liturgical instructions say and why, and then to offer a comment on where your question came from. The *General Instruction of the Roman Missal* states that a deacon or, in his absence, the lector joins the priest and other ministers in the entrance procession to the altar and that he or she "may carry the *Book of the Gospels*" (n. 120 d). It also indicates that the *Book of the Gospels* is placed on the altar when the ministers reach it in procession (n. 122) and that the priest takes it from the altar during the singing of the Alleluia before the gospel is proclaimed. Carrying the *Book of the Gospels* (as opposed to the *Lectionary for Mass*) was always envisioned as part of the Introductory Rite at Mass but the United States did not publish a gospel book separate from the *Lectionary for Mass* until the revised *General Instruction* was issued in 2002. What would be pastorally helpful today would be to place the *Lectionary* at the ambo before Mass begins, to have the readers proclaim the scriptures other than the gospel from that *Lectionary*, and then have the deacon (or priest in the deacon's absence) process with the gospel book from the altar to the ambo to proclaim the gospel.

The use of two books for the proclamation of the scriptures should not be interpreted as a separation between the Old Testament and the epistles on the one hand (from the *Lectionary*) and the gospel (from the *Book of the Gospels*) on the other. There is one revealed Word of God in both testaments, but clearly the words of Jesus in the gospels have classically received greater reverence in the church's liturgy. In addition, the use of two specially crafted and designed books can help us appreciate the symbolic value of the proclamation of the Word—from beautiful books, not sheets of paper, disposable "missals," or anything of the sort.

28. The Missal contains antiphons at the Entrance and Communion parts of the Mass. Should these be sung or said?

Antiphons are short sentences, most often from the scriptures (sometimes a paraphrase), that are in the Missal for the Entrance and Communion processions. They are meant to be interspersed through the verses of a psalm not unlike the way the Responsorial Psalm is arranged in the *Lectionary for Mass*. In the extraordinary form of the Mass (high and solemn Masses) they are always sung, and at a low Mass they are recited by the priest. With regard to the entrance antiphon, the *General Instruction of the Roman Missal* (n. 48) states that "this chant is sung alternately by the choir and the people or similarly by a cantor and the people, or entirely by the people, or by the choir alone. It is possible to use the antiphon with its Psalm from the *Graduale Romanum* or the *Graduate Simplex*, or another chant that is suited to the sacred action, the day, or the time of year, and whose text has been approved by the Conference of Bishops." In *Sing to the Lord* (n. 144), the American bishops state that "the singing of an antiphon and psalm during the entrance procession has been a long-standing tradition in the Roman Liturgy." At the end of this same section it states that "the texts of antiphons, psalms, hymns, and songs for the Liturgy must have been approved either by the United States Conference of Catholic Bishops or by the local diocesan bishop." The same phrasing is repeated for the Communion antiphons. When there is no singing, the *General Instruction of the Roman Missal* (n. 48) states that "if there is no singing at the Entrance, the antiphon given in the Missal is recited either by the faithful, or by some of them, or by a reader; otherwise, it is recited by the Priest himself, who may even adapt it as an introductory explanation."

Allow me to make two comments, one liturgical, the other (more) theological. The first point is that the use of metrical hymns (many taken from our Protestant brothers and sisters) often replaced the singing of antiphons when the Mass of Pope Paul VI was first implemented in the vernacular. This was not a surprise because we had no musical repertory to use for the English-language liturgical texts. With the passage of time, however, and the increased attention given to the antiphons as a liturgical unit, there are increasing numbers of musical settings for the antiphons that are worth singing in celebration. Also from a liturgical point of view, the length of the entrance procession dictates the length of the singing, and the interspersed psalm verses could be more or less numerous depending on the celebration. And finally from a liturgical perspective, metrical hymns are proper to the celebration of the Liturgy of the Hours. They are not proper to the Eucharist. In my judgment they can become too "heavy" at these times of the Mass when repeating what a cantor or choir intones can be simpler and "lighter."

The second point is theological. On major feasts and seasons, it is especially important to check the antiphons assigned for the Mass of the day to see what they "say" theologically and then, if the antiphon itself is not sung, to try to emulate that in what is sung. For example, at "Mass during the Night" at Christmas, the entrance antiphon is "The Lord said to me: You are my Son. It is I who have begotten you this day" (from Ps 2:7). The use of this psalm is very significant because these verses have often been used in the Catholic theological tradition to describe who Christ is. Especially on Christmas, the notion of being "begotten" of God is very rich. In and through the Incarnation all is changed, and in Christ we are related to God and God to us irrevocably and forever. The issue here is what occurs to us in and through Christ, the only begotten Son of God. It is about the Trinitarian relationship of Father, Son, and Spirit, and the

church's relationship with the Trinity in and through the Son.
Christmas is not merely about the historical event of Christ. When
the music we sing at Christmas underscores this reality of relatedness
and emphasizes that Christ, who was divine, took on humanity so
that we humans could become God (from St. Augustine), then we are
in important and rich theological territory. But if the music retells the
events that led to Christ's birth, then I think we are engaged more in
a historical retelling of this story rather than how that event changed
all of humanity then and now. In effect I judge this antiphon to be
very important over against "It Came Upon a Midnight Clear" or a
refrain like "Come let us adore him."

Another example is the Communion antiphons for the
Sundays of Lent. These antiphons are taken directly from the gospel
of the day. This provides an important reminder that Word and
Eucharist are one act of worship. It also helps to underscore what
are universally acclaimed as among the most important gospel texts
we read annually. To have a key phrase from that gospel echoed at
the Communion procession places us again in rich theological territory. Whether we sing them as is or allow them to guide our
selection of music, a review of these antiphons for Lent can go a
long way toward offering us what the church would have in our
minds and on our lips as we process to Communion during this
most holy season.

29. Why does the priest go to the chair for the beginning of Mass and not the altar?

I've spent a lot of time talking about what the liturgical rites
and texts say to discover what they mean theologically. Now I have
the chance to shift to interpreting what we mean theologically by the
placement and use of the chair, a relatively recent addition to the
arrangement of our sanctuaries. The theological meaning of the chair
as an important place from which the priest "presides" at Mass (a
term used repeatedly in the *General Instruction of the Roman Missal*,
for example, n. 5) derives from the *cathedra,* or the bishop's chair in
his diocese that is housed in the central church of the diocese, the

cathedral. The meaning of a *cathedra*, or chair, is a place that symbolizes the teaching authority of the bishop and the bishop in communion with all the bishops in the church and the pope (hence the great importance attached to a papal teaching that is *ex cathedra*, or literally "from the chair").

In the reform of the Mass, the chair was reintroduced for use at all Masses, whereas in the Tridentine solemn high Mass the priest, deacon, and subdeacon use a side bench when they are not at the altar. So the regular use of the chair is not new: it's a restoration to an older practice that we now use regularly. The theological reasoning behind its use is to differentiate the parts of the Mass by location, not just description. According to all post–Vatican II statements about the Mass, its two essential parts are the Liturgy of the Word and the Liturgy of the Eucharist, which are so closely connected as to be one act of worship. Now the priest may preach the homily from the chair, as a symbol of teaching authority. (It is interesting that the *General Instruction of the Roman Missal*, n. 135, states explicitly: "The priest, standing at the chair or at the ambo itself, or when appropriate, in another suitable place, gives the homily.") However, more commonly in America, he chooses to stand at the ambo as most people do when delivering speeches. More common (and required) is the use of the chair from which the priest leads the introductory and concluding rites of the Mass. He returns to the chair after the homily to lead the Profession of Faith and to introduce and conclude the intercessions. This location differentiates these parts of the Mass from the primary and truly essential parts: the Word proclaimed from the ambo and the Eucharist from the altar table.

30. The Mass always starts joyfully with song and prayer, but then we move to a somber Penitential Rite. Why the sudden change?

This is a frequently asked question and an issue that causes some confusion. The *General Instruction* (n. 24) states that the Act of

Penitence is one element of the Introductory Rites, which are "the Entrance, Greeting, Act of Penitence, *Kyrie, Gloria,* and Collect [which together] have the character of a beginning, introduction, and preparation." Then it goes on to say (as I noted in the response to question 25) that "their purpose is to ensure that the faithful who come together as one, establish communion and dispose themselves properly to listen to the word of God and to celebrate the Eucharist worthily."

About the Act of Penitence specifically, the *General Instruction of the Roman Missal* (n. 51) states:

> The Priest calls upon the whole community to take part in the Penitential Act, which, after a brief pause for silence, it does by means of a formula of general confession. The rite concludes with the Priest's absolution, which, however, lacks the efficacy of the Sacrament of Penance.
>
> From time to time on Sundays, especially in Easter Time, instead of the customary Penitential Act, the blessing and sprinkling of water may take place as a reminder of Baptism.

I suspect from your question that the key word in this description is *confession* since the Penitential Rite does acknowledge our sinfulness and unworthiness before God, especially through such phrases as having sinned "through my most grievous fault" in the prayer beginning "I confess." But the word *confess* also means to declare our faith publicly: the church sometimes even calls certain people "confessors" because they did this in an extraordinary way. So even when we acknowledge our sins, it is with a sense of expressing our faith in God and our thanks to God for forgiveness.

Structurally it is also important to see that in the present form of the Act of Penitence, there are three options (a fourth option, the blessing with holy water, is addressed in the next question). Each of these is introduced by the priest. The first choice is the traditional "I confess" prayer, which in the Roman Missal reads "in what I have done and in what I have failed to do." Hence, it couples admission of sin before God with an admission of our sinfulness in not responding to the needs of others. The second option for the Penitential Act simply names that we have sinned and asks for God's mercy and salvation. The third form is a variation on the "Lord, have mercy" litany, from the Greek *Kyrie eleison*. The sense of the Greek original is not that we strike our breasts and act as though we are "sinners in the hands of an angry God." Rather, the sense of the Greek is an acclamation proclaiming God as the ever-merciful God on whom we can rely and whose allegiance we profess at the Eucharist. The Roman Missal contains one set of three invocations for God's mercy—"to heal the contrite," "to call sinners," and "you are seated at the right hand of the Father…."—but they are not assertions about sins or failures.

The Appendix to the Missal contains several additional sets of invocations, again always focused on attributes of Christ. It would be helpful to review them to see how they reflect different times of the liturgical year and what invocations might be appropriate for a given feast or season. Again the principle in evidence is of admitting sinfulness in the light of God's forgiving and reconciling love. This last option, the rather familiar threefold statements about attributes and names for Christ, is the most important theologically because through it we profess faith in who Christ is and what he now does for us at the liturgy. In no way are they statements about what we have done wrong. From this evidence of background and present texts in the Roman Missal, I'd reply that while the Act of Penitence is part of the introduction to the Mass it should not be understood as overly negative and focused only on sin. It is a communal action whereby we admit our need for God's grace through his Son at the Eucharist we celebrate. Our admission of sin is clearly personal but also prayed with others who are equally human and fallible, and who fall into sin. If we think that the Penitential Rite is becoming too narrowly focused on our individual sins or on guilt, check the wording of the Missal and see whether what you are hearing is what is there.

31. Why at some Masses do we renew our baptismal vows?

I'm sure you have noticed that traditionally the Catholic Church places holy water fonts at the church entrances and that baptisteries were (and sometimes still are) located near the rear doors of the church (to signify admission into the community of the baptized). Given the present reform of the liturgy, the baptismal fonts have often been moved to a place of great prominence (normally near the church door), and people are now encouraged to bless themselves not only from holy water fonts but from the baptismal font itself. The theological meaning of this is clear: every Eucharist is a commemoration and a renewal of the covenant of baptism.

It was because the renewal of baptismal vows was only done in the extraordinary form at the (solemn) high Mass that the church began using holy water fonts so people could bless themselves whenever they entered the church to signify the connection between baptism and Eucharist. However, with the present reformed Eucharistic Liturgy, we now have the option of using the blessing and sprinkling with water as part of the Introductory Rites at Sunday Mass. We should pay close attention to this prayer because it gives us a brief overview of salvation history and our sharing in God's eternal salvation through the sacred signs of water at baptism and of bread and wine at the Eucharist. On Sundays, the day of Christ's rising to new life after his death on the cross, this is clearly a preferable option with which to begin the Eucharist, especially during the Easter season, because it signifies how Sunday Eucharist is the premier liturgical action whereby we renew our baptismal covenant and deepen our conversion to Christ.

In the extraordinary form this rite is known as the *Asperges me* ("you will sprinkle water upon me"), which phrase is from the psalm that was traditionally used to accompany the sprinkling itself (Ps 50:9). In the present reform, this same psalm can be used, as can another antiphon or appropriate song. The theological point here is that through the symbol of water, the texts of the introduction, the blessing prayer, the act of sprinkling, and the singing of an appropriate antiphon, we renew our baptismal commitment both at the beginning of the Eucharist and through the whole Eucharist itself.

32. In the beginning of Mass, there is a prayer called the Collect. Where does the term *Collect* come from? What does it mean?

The *General Instruction of the Roman Missal* (n. 54) states that "the Priest calls upon the people to pray and everybody, together with the Priest, observes a brief silence so that they may become aware of being in God's presence and may call to mind their intentions. Then the Priest pronounces the prayer usually called the 'Collect' and through which the character of the celebration finds expression." The silent pause before the prayer is said aloud allows us to silently form our intentions for the Mass (that is, call to mind our needs and hopes). Such pauses are very helpful to underscore how the Mass is communal and public, an act we participate in, and yet also contains some times for personal reflection and prayer. (In fact, some liturgical commentators say that this pause for personal prayer is the *real* Collect and that what follows is an addition, a more general prayer.)

Now history reveals some interesting background to the notion of the *collect*. On special feast days and during certain seasons, the liturgy in Rome included "station Masses," meaning the pope would travel to various churches, or "stations," throughout the city for Mass. (The devotional practice of station Masses eventually extended to other larger cities and dioceses.) During Lent this custom included a procession from a gathering place (most often a church) to the church where the Mass was to be celebrated. The ministers and the faithful would join in a penitential procession behind a relic of the true cross. At the time that they gathered for the procession, a prayer would be prayed *ad collectam*, meaning a prayer at the place of gathering. Then when the pope (or priest) arrived at the church for Mass, he would then pray another Collect, or opening prayer. When this custom of praying two Collects and processing to church for Mass died out, the opening prayer was called a "Collect" and we were encouraged to "collect" our intentions for the Mass.

You will notice that the Collect prayer is short: an address to God and a petition of God. Sometimes it refers to the feast or season being celebrated. At other times, it is a very general acknowledgment of our need for God's mercy. On weekdays that are not special feasts or seasons, the priest may choose the opening prayer from a number of options in the Missal under "Masses and Prayers for Various Needs and Occasions." Or he may use any of the prayers assigned for the Sundays in Ordinary Time. Careful selection of these options can enhance daily celebrations and prevent them from becoming routine by the proclamation of the same prayers.

V

Liturgy of the Word

33. Who decides the cycle of readings in the *Lectionary for Mass* and why?

Your question is straightforward and direct but not that easy to answer. The simple answer would be the Vatican under the auspices of the Sacred Congregation for Divine Worship. But that is still rather vague. You see, the reforms of the liturgy after Vatican II were anonymous in the sense that they were officially endorsed by the popes at the time (and therefore had the highest authority of the church behind them), but we do not always know exactly who did what "behind the scenes." Let me try to explain.

The Liturgy Constitution of Vatican II was the clarion call for the reform of all the rites of the Roman liturgy. It also contained the first official directives indicating the scope of the reforms to be undertaken. As for the reform of the readings at Mass, the Liturgy Constitution states that "the treasures of the bible are to be opened up more lavishly, so that richer fare may be provided for the faithful at the table of God's Word. In this way a more representative portion of the holy scriptures will be read to the people in the course of a prescribed number of years" (n. 51). As with the reform of all the other parts of the liturgy, the task of revising the readings for Mass was entrusted to a study group of the Vatican agency responsible for the reform (called the *Consilium*). According to the secretary for that body, Archbishop Annibale Bugnini, this was "one of the most difficult tasks of the entire reform: the reorganization of the readings for Mass." Because Archbishop Bugnini had firsthand knowledge of the process of the reform (and wrote about it), we know that the two chief architects of this work were Fathers Gaston Fontaine (Canada) and Cipriano Vagaggini (Italy). Father Vagaggini was very involved at every step of the process of preparing the Liturgy Constitution and the reform of many parts of the liturgy while Father Fontaine surrendered his post in Canada in 1964 to be at the disposal of the *Consilium*, largely to work on the lectionary.

The basis of the *Consilium's* lectionary work was a study of the arrangement of readings that have been used for Mass from the patristic times through the Middle Ages and, of course, the previous structure of readings in the Tridentine Mass. Some of their sources were lists of texts, other sources were actual books of readings—lectionaries and gospel books. In the Tridentine (extraordinary) form of the Mass, we use a Missal that contains all the prayers and readings for Mass. In the earlier centuries of the church's life, however, the lectionaries and gospel books were separate books of scripture readings. Similarly, the sacramentary was the book containing the prayers of the Mass said by the priest; the antiphonal was the book containing the chants sung by the schola, choir, and congregation; and so on. All these were compressed into one book, the Missal, when the other ministers and ministries at Mass were taken over by the priest himself, and he did all the parts of the Mass himself.

With the restoration at Vatican II of the variety of roles in the liturgy, the decision was made to return to the former practice of having several books for the celebration of Mass. The *Lectionary for Mass*, therefore, contains the readings only. The *Book of the Gospels* contains the gospel readings only for Sundays and solemnities. The study group assigned to the task of reforming the list of scripture readings therefore made several decisions about the contents of the lectionary and the gospel book as liturgical books. Very often the readings were chosen to reflect the feast being celebrated, for example, the resurrection gospels for Easter or the accounts of Christ's birth for Midnight Mass at Christmas. The answer to the next question can help fill out details about the present shape of our lectionary.

34. Can you help me understand the structure of the *Lectionary*—both for Sundays and for weekdays?

Generally, we can say that there are two sets of readings for weekday Masses and three sets for Sundays in what we call either Ordinary Time or the "season" of the year, meaning Advent,

Christmas, Lent, and Easter. My term *set of readings* is more often than not referred to in the literature on the present liturgy as a "cycle" of readings for Sundays and as the "year" for weekdays, but whatever term is used, the point is the same.

Now let me try to break down your question into three responses, lest this get all too confusing.

Ordinary Time—Sundays. For every Sunday in Ordinary Time in the liturgical year, three scripture readings are assigned—Old Testament, New Testament, and gospel—according to a plan whereby one set of readings on a given Sunday is proclaimed once every three years. The plan for the three sets of readings is such that each of the Synoptic Gospels (Matthew, Mark, and Luke) is proclaimed in a given calendar year—hence the reference you sometimes see to the first cycle (Year A) as the year of Matthew; the second cycle (Year B) as the year of Mark; and the third cycle (Year C) as the year of Luke. Over the thirty or so weeks that make up Ordinary Time, each of these gospels is proclaimed in order, which is called the continuous reading of the gospel (the Latin term is *lectio continua*). The first reading for all these Sundays is from the Old Testament, and the particular text chosen for a particular Sunday is determined by the fact that it is judged to be an echo of or a prelude to what the gospel proclaims. What follows, the Responsorial Psalm, is meant to be a prayerful reiteration of that first reading (and should be sung because the psalms are songs). That means that there is a thematic unity among the gospel, Old Testament, and psalm for Ordinary Time Sundays. The second reading is taken from the epistles of St. Paul and sections of these letters are proclaimed in order (like the gospels, a *lectio continua*). Therefore, on each Sunday in Ordinary Time you have two major themes from the readings that can be the basis for the homily that day.

Ordinary Time—Weekdays. On the weekdays of Ordinary Time, you have a similar continuous reading of the gospels each day, but for weekdays we hear all the Synoptic Gospels read in order over the course of one year. The *Lectionary for Mass* gives us the Gospel of Mark from the first week of Ordinary Time through the ninth week, the Gospel of Matthew from the tenth week through the twenty-first week, and the Gospel of Luke from the twenty-second week through the thirty-third week. Now, when it comes to the first reading on weekdays of Ordinary Time, the texts selected are chosen to allow a continuous reading of a book of the Bible other than the gospels, again in order. But like the arrangement for Sundays, the psalm is chosen to be a prayerful reiteration of that first reading. The reason I said that there are two sets of weekday readings is because each set of the first reading is proclaimed on alternate years, while the gospel is the same every year. (These first readings are referred to as Year I and Year II.)

Seasons. When it comes to the special seasons of Advent, Christmas, Lent, and Easter, the familiar pattern of three readings on Sundays remains. The choice of precisely which readings and why depends on a number of factors and all of it is explained in the Introduction to the *Lectionary for Mass.* Let me give one example. In the season of Lent, on the first Sunday in all three years of the *Lectionary*, all the gospels are about Jesus' temptation (from the Synoptics), and on the second Sunday, the gospels recount his transfiguration (again from the Synoptics). What happens for the next three weeks in the A cycle, however, is a shift to the Gospel of John, chapters 4, 9, and 11. These three texts proclaim the dialogue of Jesus with the Samaritan woman (John 4), the cure of the man born blind (John 9), and the raising of the dead man Lazarus (John 11). The reason why these gospels are specially chosen is simultaneously traditional and theological. From the fourth century on, these texts were chosen to be proclaimed during Lent to remind those already baptized and to let those to be baptized at Easter know what baptism means—new life in Christ. Hence, the symbol of water (the Samaritan woman at the well), the symbol of light (the blind man now able to see), and the notion of real life through faith in Jesus (the dead man Lazarus raised up) that are proclaimed on these Sundays are the very symbols used at baptism at the Easter Vigil when the elect are baptized and candidates make their faith profession in the Catholic Church.

This notion of history and theology is also operative in the way much of the *Lectionary* for these same seasons has come about. For example, the scripture readings during the weekdays of Lent are the same each year, and stress themes related to baptism, reconciliation, and identification with the paschal dying and rising of Christ. In the season of Easter, as you probably have noticed, we never read the Old Testament and the gospels are always from John. Why? Liturgical tradition insists that in Christ we are a new creation and the old covenant cedes its emphasis to the new covenant in Christ in a special way during this season. Hence, during the whole Easter season, the first reading is from the Acts of the Apostles to show how the risen Christ worked in the early church and continues to work among us now. The Gospel of John was chosen because, from the time of St. Irenaeus, it was regarded as "the spiritual gospel," much less concerned with details of Jesus' earthly life than with how we are identified with Christ and abide in God through him. We proclaim it for the fifty days of Easter to deepen our experience of our life in the risen Christ.

I hope all this isn't too confusing! Simply put, there is a rhyme and reason to the *Lectionary*. What's the best way to understand it? I'd recommend that you read the Introduction of the *Lectionary* to understand the rationale for the texts selected and insight into the theological meaning of the proclamation of the scriptures at Mass. Second, I'd recommend that you review and pray over the scripture readings for the following Sunday (and weekdays too) in order to get a sense of their breadth and implications for your life here and now. It is impossible to really experience the fullness of the readings at Mass without this preparation. After a while I'm sure the mechanics of what I have tried to explain will become both clear and less important, and the experience of applying the scriptures to your life and living more completely in God will happen.

35. Is it true that Protestant churches proclaim the same readings we do on Sundays? What does this mean ecumenically?

At the same time that Pope Paul VI endorsed and officially sanctioned the use of the Roman Missal revised after Vatican II (1969), he officially endorsed the *Lectionary for Mass*, which contains perhaps the most far-reaching organization of biblical readings for Mass that the Catholic Church has ever had. A very significant outgrowth of its adoption by our church has been its adoption (more or less) by a number of other Christian churches. So it was on a recent Sunday morning that at the eucharistic liturgies celebrated by members of neighboring Catholic, Episcopal, Lutheran, and Presbyterian, as well as some Methodist and Disciples of Christ Churches, all listened to the same passages from the scriptures. Therefore, you are quite right to point out the ecumenical implications of this phenomenon, one not directly planned, but a very significant outgrowth of the Second Vatican Council. How did this "quiet ecumenism" come about?

In 1978, the (North American) Consultation on Common Texts set to work on determining a more or less common set of scripture readings for Sundays that Christian churches could adopt. The resulting *Common Lectionary* was published in 1982, and a decade later a revised set of readings was published as *The Revised Common Lectionary*. These lectionaries are based on the Roman Catholic *Lectionary* and the discussions that led to the publication of these lectionaries had Roman Catholics as participants in the process.

An underlying principle of liturgical study (which I have repeatedly used in this book) is *lex orandi, lex credendi*—what we pray shapes what we believe. Now this is true not just for the prayers of the Mass but also for the scriptures we proclaim. As the Catholic Church still strives to reemphasize the value of biblical proclamation at Mass (and at all liturgies), the fact that we have such similar lectionary structures can only help to enhance our spiritual and theological ties across the lines of our various denom-inations. If it is true that "the family that prays together, stays together," who knows what ecumenical ties will be fostered by churches that pray over the same biblical readings week after week?

36. Which readings are required and which are optional? For example, my wife and I chose the readings for our wedding, but the Sunday scriptures seem to be required.

One of the most important features of the present lectionary structure for Mass is that it provides scripture readings for every day of the year, and unless there are important exceptions (which I'll soon describe), the readings are required and are not optional (see Introduction of the *Lectionary for Mass*, nn. 78–80). Sometimes dur-ing the week a special feast day occurs with scripture readings that are specially chosen for that day (for example, the ascension or the feast of St. John the Baptist). On these days the special readings take the place of those in the weekday lectionary. When this occurs, the priest should look ahead to the whole week's readings to determine whether the daily readings that are omitted for that special feast day should be combined and proclaimed together with the weekday readings the day before or after the feast (see *Lectionary*, Introduction, n. 82).

Perhaps an illustration is the best way to make my point. As I mentioned in my answer to question 34, each of the Synoptic Gospels is proclaimed on the weekdays in Ordinary Time. Let's say that while we are proclaiming the Gospel of Matthew in the week-day lectionary, the readings assigned for a special feast are to super-sede the proclamation of the Beatitudes (Matt 5) assigned to that weekday. If this occurs, the priest would want to proclaim the Beatitudes in conjunction with the assigned gospel of the day before or after the feast, so that what is proclaimed during the rest of that section of Matthew's Gospel that week based on the Beatitudes can lead to how they can be the better understood.

However, there are occasions, like your wedding, for which we can use "ritual Masses," when other scripture texts can be chosen that replace the weekday readings. In this case you would have the opportunity to choose from a lectionary of readings that has been prepared for weddings (just as there are lectionaries for baptisms, ordinations, religious profession, funerals, and more), so that the scriptures proclaimed for that ritual Mass reflect the specific sacrament being celebrated. But even here, on the Sundays of the special seasons of Advent, Christmas, Lent, and Easter, the scripture readings assigned for those Sundays during those seasons cannot be changed. The reason? The scripture readings for those seasons are specially selected and are extremely important for the whole church's celebration of the fullness of Christmas and Easter.

37. In what way should the psalm be considered responsorial, and is it supposed to be sung?

Allow me to cite two famous church fathers and a contemporary church document to answer your question. The notion that the psalm after the first reading is responsorial and that the congregation should "respond" to the cantor is found in the liturgical writings of St. Augustine in the early fifth century. But by the end of the sixth century it had become a virtuoso piece to be sung by the deacon only! Therefore, in 595, St. Gregory the Great forbade this solo singing. As choirs and scholas took over most of the people's sung participation in the Mass, this psalm was reduced to a couple of verses (called the Gradual) and was regularly combined with the Alleluia before the gospel. The Introduction of the *Lectionary for Mass* cites this as an important, integral element of the Word of God (n. 19) and stresses that every means available should be used to facilitate the congregation's singing (n. 21). This Introduction states that the psalm is led by the cantor or psalmist from the lectern, which location shows its importance as part of the Liturgy of the Word.

The *Lectionary for Mass* presumes that the psalm is sung and offers two options. Either it is sung by the cantor with the congregation repeating the sung refrain after each verse or it can be sung straight through, either by the cantor alone or by the congregation together. The only exception to this preferred practice is found in the same Introduction (n. 22), which states that "when not sung, the responsorial psalm is to be recited in a manner conducive to meditation on the Word of God."

Let me make a final comment on the psalm's importance. The restoration of the proclamation of the scriptures at Mass in the vernacular is for the spiritual benefit of the whole church. In a literal and figurative sense, the Book of Psalms is the church's prayer book. It contains the range of human emotions and reflects the spiritual ups and downs that believers always experience. The psalms are both Israel's and the Christian church's sung prayer. They were originally set to music and should be sung. As a part of the Liturgy of the Word, one advantage of the sung psalm is that it provides a change from the spoken proclamation of the readings and offers the congregation the opportunity to reflect about what had been proclaimed through song and personal prayer.

In theory, the other sung parts of the Mass of the Roman Rite for Mass (Entrance, Offertory, and Communion) are taken from the psalms. In practice, however, to facilitate easier participation by the congregation, the American bishops allowed the use of other hymns or songs (see answer to question 28) with which the people are familiar as a substitute for the singing of psalms at these parts of the liturgy. However, the Responsorial Psalm is not to be replaced by any other song (most recently reiterated in *Sing to the Lord*, n. 159); because it may be the only psalm that the congregation sings and hears, it has even greater importance than if it were one of four psalms sung at Mass.

The bottom line? Follow Augustine and Gregory and you can't go wrong!

38. What is the Gospel Acclamation and is it required?

The purpose of the Gospel Acclamation is to set up or introduce the proclamation of the gospel that follows it. It introduces the good news of the words and deeds of Christ. In all the seasons of the church year except for Lent (which does not use the Alleluia from Ash Wednesday until the Easter Vigil), this part of the Mass is commonly called the Alleluia. Structurally it normally consists of the Alleluia first sung by the cantor or choir, repeated by everyone, a verse from scripture sung by the cantor or choir, and a final Alleluia sung by all. The source of the scripture verse varies. More often than not on Sundays, this verse is taken from one of the verses in the gospel that follows. *Sing to the Lord* states:

> When there is only one reading before the gospel, the Gospel Acclamation may be omitted; if it is a season in which the *Alleluia* is said, the *Alleluia* may be used as the response of the Psalm, or the Psalm with its proper response may be used followed by the *Alleluia* with its verse. The Gospel Acclamation may be omitted if it is not sung. (n. 164)

Before I conclude answering this question, it is important to add that the use of periods of silence after the readings is a very important part of the Liturgy of the Word. The dynamic at work should be proclamation with attentive listening, silence, and sung response. My own experience is that if communities have not regularly engaged in silence after the readings, once introduced it becomes a most welcome part of their personal appropriation of the readings and of their liturgical participation in general.

39. Do we have to have a Children's Liturgy of the Word? Is it correct to have a Children's Mass instead? If not, why not?

I've already referred to the important document from 1973 called the *Directory for Masses with Children* as a major contribution to the liturgical formation that children can and should receive about the Mass and about their particular participation in the Mass. One of the principal advantages of this liturgical document is that it is not just a "how to" set of norms. Rather it is like the other general instructions to all the revised liturgical rites because it contains a generous section (chapter 1) on the liturgical, catechetical, and pedagogical value of involving children in the liturgy. The document describes two common pastoral situations. One describes Masses with adults in which children participate (chapter 2). It is in this section that you will find a description of a Liturgy of the Word, including the homily, with the children in a separate room from the body of the church (n. 17). This document has led many parishes to have a separate Liturgy of the Word for children at a Sunday Mass. The consistent principle in the *Directory*, however, is that the children should be instructed in how to participate in the regular Mass and that they should be made to feel a part of the assembly. This can happen when the priest addresses them specifically in some comments during the Mass (for example, the introduction to Mass or before the readings), in some petitions to the intercessions, and even in a part of the homily at Masses when the children are not separated from the adults for the Liturgy of the Word. The children return to the main Sunday assembly at the Presentation of the Gifts and remain with their parents for the rest of the Mass.

The second pastoral situation envisioned by the *Directory* is at Masses with children in which only a few adults participate. The document presumes that this circumstance occurs normally on weekdays (n. 20). The document reiterates the important principle that even when parts of the Mass are adapted to the children, "it is always necessary to keep in mind that these eucharistic celebrations must lead toward the celebration of Mass with adults" (n. 21). It is in this section of the document about these celebrations that we find the statement that "one of the adults may speak to the children after the gospel, especially if the priest finds it difficult to adapt himself to the mentality of the children" (n. 24).

In my experience, the "problem" with a special Liturgy of the Word for children or with Masses specially planned and celebrated for them is not the theory, it's what happens in practice. Sometimes because of a lack of resources, or even a lack of appreciating what

a *Liturgy* of the Word is, what can happen is that children leave the
congregation for what resembles instruction on the scriptures and
an activity like coloring. This can easily happen if they are dismissed to a classroom. This is where some parishes that have daily
Mass chapels are at an advantage and can dismiss the children there.
What we need to recall is the importance that the *Directory* places
on this special Liturgy of the Word as a *liturgy*, which means an
event that involves the children in listening, singing, praying in
silence, and offering petitions in the intercessions. Since the aim is
to progressively engage them in the regular adult Mass, the more
we can mirror the regular structure of the Sunday Mass at these
special Liturgies of the Word, the better.

40. Why do some people trace the cross on their foreheads, lips, and hearts at the gospel?

This ritual gesture is not found in the ritual description of
the Order of Mass. The present Missal states that at the proclamation of the gospel, the deacon (or priest if there is no deacon) sings
or says, "A reading from the holy Gospel according to…," and then
"makes the sign of the cross on the book, and then on his forehead,
lips, and breast." The meaning of at least part of this is taken from
the blessing that the priest gives to the deacon (or which the priest
says to himself if there is no deacon): "May the Lord be in your
heart and on your lips that you may proclaim his Gospel worthily
and well." This gesture is important as a nonverbal reminder to the
one who proclaims the gospel that it is indeed good news and that
in proclaiming this text, the deacon or priest should revere its message in what he thinks (mind), in what he says (lips), and in his
heart (breast). The fact that many in the congregation imitate this
gesture may well signal their own willingness to do the same thing.
Even though it is not prescribed for the congregation, it is not
something that I'd take away from them. After all, liturgy involves
gestures and movement and this addition to the congregation's participation seems quite logical and legitimate.

41. Our priest announced that Sunday's homily at all Masses will be dramatized by the youth group. We do the same on Christmas Eve. Is this correct? And what's the difference between a sermon and a homily?

Let me take the second part of your question first. The term *homily* comes from the Greek word *homilia* and refers to speech that is more familiar and "true to life" than the language of high rhetoric often associated with classical oratory. It is a term that has been recovered with the reform of the liturgy to indicate the kind of public speech that follows the proclamation of the gospel. The homily is intended to explain "the biblical word of God proclaimed in the readings or some other texts of the liturgy [and] must always lead the community of the faithful to celebrate the eucharist wholeheartedly" (*Lectionary*, Introduction, n. 24). It is recommended that it be well prepared, not too long or too short, and suited to all those present, even children and the uneducated (n. 24). Now that's a tall order! And what a challenge for the presiding priest who (normally) is the one to deliver it.

Strictly speaking, therefore, the homily is not a sermon, since the subject matter for sermons is any kind of religious theme. Similarly, a dramatization at the homily would not seem to fit the criteria just cited. Let's take the example of Christmas Eve. Often what happens is the dramatization of the Christmas story. This means that as the gospel is proclaimed, young people especially act out or dramatize what we are hearing. Sometimes what happens is that after the gospel a dramatization of the events of Christ's birth at Bethlehem occurs, sometimes with a script that echoes the gospel. Or this involves the people engaged in speaking and acting out their parts. Now the problem with such dramatizations is not the medium so much as it is the message. The purpose of the homily is to draw out the message of the good news for us here and now. The homily follows the gospel as its extension, its application. It is not meant to be a repetition or summary of what we have already heard. It is intended to help us penetrate and experience more fully what we have already heard and to lead us to celebrate the Eucharist that follows wholeheartedly. Dramatizations can be legitimate vehicles for catechesis or instruction about the gospels. But they do not serve the liturgy because they "freeze the frame" on what happened in history, whereas the purpose of the homily is to help us experience God's saving good news here and now.

Pastorally what often lies behind the dramatization in the homily is that this affords a way for the youth to be more fully involved in the Mass. My recommendation in such a case is to involve the youth in a number of ways in the liturgy itself and in preparing for it. There is nothing that says that all liturgical roles are reserved for people over a certain age. Having young people involved in music ministry, in reading, in offering petitions for the Prayer of the Faithful, in serving at the altar, and so on, can enhance their participation and experience of the liturgy. The only caution I would offer is that roles are meant to serve the liturgy, and those chosen to fulfill them should be able to do so, for example, those who read should have that ability. Anything childish or that detracts from the beauty and flow of the liturgy should be avoided. Regarding participation, involving some young people in a group that helps the priest prepare the homily can help the final result to resonate more fully with the lived experience of the community. And that, after all, is one of the most important aspects of what homily preparation and execution is all about!

42. Is there really a difference between when the scriptures are read in the liturgy and when I pray over them at home?

Your question is very focused and reflects a deepening appreciation for the proclamation of the Word as an essential part of the way we experience Christ's salvation in the Mass. But to answer it, let me use an example from the Book of Genesis to affirm that, yes, there is a difference. In the first chapter of Genesis, we read of the way God created the heavens and the earth during the seven days of creation—it was by God's speaking that things came to be. Take the first day when God created light: "And God said, 'Let there be light,' and there was light" (vs. 3). It's as simple and yet as profound as that. God speaks and things happen. The Liturgy of the Word is essentially an action of divine address and our response to it where the scriptures are proclaimed. In the act of being proclaimed, they reveal God's divine plans and irrevocable covenant, and in the act of proclamation, they make that covenant operative for us here and now.

Another example is from the beginning of Jesus' public ministry in Luke's Gospel. In chapter 4, Jesus returns to Nazareth, enters the synagogue, proclaims the text from Isaiah about the suffering servant (Isa 61:1–2), and then declares, "Today this scripture passage is fulfilled in your hearing" (Luke 4:21). Whenever we proclaim the scriptures, what is described is fulfilled in our hearing. What the text proclaims about the words and deeds of Jesus happens to and for us now. In other words, what happens when the scriptures are proclaimed is an event of salvation, not just a description of salvation. The proclaimed scriptures are our present experience of covenant relatedness to God through Christ, not just a description of what the covenant is like.

The very structure of the Liturgy of the Word reveals how we understand that it is an event of our salvation. In the liturgy we engage in a dialogue. God speaks through the scriptures and we accept and commit ourselves to them by saying, "Thanks be to God," or "Praise to you, Lord Jesus Christ." The divine address to us through the Word invites our human response of acceptance and commitment. We do this through the acclamations at the end of each proclaimed text, the Responsorial Psalm, and the Gospel Acclamation. One of the purposes of the homily is to draw out some aspect of the proclamation of the scriptures and apply this good news to our needs and lives here and now.

Take the example of the parable of the prodigal son from Luke 15. This text is now used in our present *Lectionary for Mass* as well as in the Liturgy of the Word for communal penance services. Every time we hear this parable proclaimed in the liturgy, God's act of acceptance, forgiveness, and reconciliation happens. What the father does for his son in the parable is what God does for us in Christ through our hearing of this parable. The kingdom of God—God's designs and actions on our behalf—is incarnate through the Word proclaimed and ratified in the eucharistic meal we share. The way we communicate as humans—through both words and gestures—is the way we experience God's salvation in the Mass.

Two comments about the rite for the proclamation of the gospel may help illustrate this. At the end of the gospel, the deacon or priest kisses the gospel book. When he does so, he says to himself, "Through the words of the Gospel may our sins be wiped away." This is a brief reminder of what it means that the gospel is proclaimed—we experience salvation again and again. A second example is from the Latin introduction to the (former) *Lectionary*. Each gospel passage was introduced by the Latin phrase *in illo tempore*, commonly translated as "at that time." That looks like a reference to when Jesus originally said or did what the gospel describes. In fact, it's the opposite. To declare "at that time" means that what Jesus did once in saving history, he does here and now for us. This little phrase was a constant reminder that the gospels are not descriptions of historical reminiscences. Rather, they are one of the privileged ways that we continue to live in God's covenant love.

In his post-synodal exhortation on the Word of God in the Life and Mission of the Church, entitled *Verbum Domini*, Pope Benedict XVI asserts (n. 52) that the church is "the home of the word" and that attention must first be given to the sacred liturgy, "for the liturgy is the privileged setting in which God speaks to us in the midst of our lives; he speaks today to his people, who hear and respond." While the entire exhortation is worth careful study and prayerful reflection, numbers 52 to 71 are particularly relevant to our purpose as they deal with the "Liturgy: Privileged Setting for the Word of God."

Now with all of this said, you may be thinking that I am neglecting or ignoring the value of praying over the scriptures in solitude. Not at all. In fact, one of the most important revolutions to have taken place in our church since Vatican II has been the way people have taken to reading and praying over the scriptures, individually and in groups. The ancient term for this is *lectio divina*, meaning a holy reading of the Bible. This kind of personal prayer is essential for us to experience the Liturgy of the Word for what it truly is. We need to know the stories of the scriptures through personal prayer in order to take them to heart as fully as possible through the Liturgy of the Word. Personal reflection on the scriptures gives us the foundation to appreciate even more fully what happens when the scriptures are proclaimed at Mass. Again I refer to *Verbum Domini* (n. 86) where the pope discusses "The Prayerful Reading of Sacred Scripture and '*Lectio Divina*.'"

43. Is the Creed always necessary at Mass?

The present Roman Rite prescribes the Profession of Faith at Masses on Sundays and solemnities. The text of the Creed is a combination of the faith professions from the Council of Nicea (325) and from Constantinople (381). More commonly it is referred to as the "Nicene Creed." At Masses with children, the simpler Apostles' Creed may be said. Here is the liturgical background: the Profession of Faith in Father, Son, and Spirit formed the baptismal question-and-answer dialogue with those to be baptized. The inclusion of the full text of the Creed started in parts of Europe as a reaction to heresies about the divinity of Christ as early as the fifth century. It was incorporated into the Roman Mass in the eleventh century.

In the present Roman Mass, the Creed is not used at the Easter Vigil because the community professes its faith through the baptismal question-and-answer form used by those being initiated and received into the church that night. On Easter Sunday itself, the Nicene Creed is usually replaced by the same dialogue question-and-answer form of the Profession of Faith from the Easter Vigil Mass.

44. Are the General Intercessions the same as the Universal Prayer and the Prayer of the Faithful? Who writes these?

The simple answer to the first part of your question is yes. In the revised Missal, the term *Universal Prayer* is the preferred term. But in effect the Universal Prayer, General Intercessions, and Prayer of the Faithful refer to the same thing. Here a little historical background might help. The Prayer of the Faithful was used to distinguish these prayers as being said by the already baptized as opposed to the catechumens, who were not yet among "the faithful" and hence were not present for these prayers. The more common terms today, *Universal Prayer* and *General Intercessions*, signify that these are prayers for the whole church and for the church as it intercedes for the whole world.

The structure of the prayer that we commonly use at Mass contains an introduction by the priest (a variation on "let us pray," not itself a prayer to God), the statement of petitions and the congregation's response, and a concluding prayer by the priest. Classically it was the deacon who announced the intentions because it was he who knew the particular needs of the community (who needed food or charity, who was sick, who had died). By exercising this liturgical role, he reflected his ministry outside the Mass and thereby exemplified the unity of worship and Christian living.

As for who "writes them," there can be a number of answers. The Introduction of the *Lectionary for Mass* states that "the deacon, another minister, or some of the faithful may propose intentions that are short and phrased with a measure of flexibility" (n. 30). What is envisioned here is the involvement of the assembly in articulating petitions, whether spoken or written down. Some parishes enlist the aid of laypeople in preparing the petitions in liturgy planning meetings; others have a box for people to drop them off as they enter church on Sunday; and some assign the task of composing them to a committee. Sometimes, however, for the sake of convenience, the priest or deacon writes the Prayer of the Faithful.

Certainly the letter of the recommendations in the Introduction of the *Lectionary* and the spirit of the prayer as the "Prayer of the Faithful" would seem to invite as much participation "of the faithful" in preparing these prayers as possible.

A number of publishers offer prepared texts for homilies and Prayers of the Faithful. In general I think that such could be helpful as background material. But in the end I think that the opportunity and discipline of writing them with a particular liturgical community's needs (strengths and weaknesses) in mind is optimum. Again, I suggest a "less is more" attitude regarding the use of words. A careful author can help address the unintended consequences of liturgies with too many words.

The Appendix to the Roman Missal includes eleven sets of sample intercessions that coincide with the liturgical seasons that are very helpful models for the General Intercessions. Normally these prayers concern the needs of the church, of the nation or world, of those suffering for any particular reason, of the sick, and finally, of the deceased. The more universal and general this prayer is, the better—hence the prayers for the nation and the world. It is interesting to note that in these sample sets of petitions, the pope is named in only two of them and the diocesan bishop is named in only one. The rest of the sample petitions are about the universal church itself. And yet how often do actual petitions name both pope and bishop? Almost always. My assessment is that it is because the pope and diocesan bishop are named in every Mass in the Eucharistic Prayer, the traditional place where they are prayed for.

When it comes to praying for the sick and the deceased, a lot depends on the size of the community and the number who are sick. I know of parishes that name all those who are sick and have asked for prayers. Sometimes, because the number can be very large, those named publicly in the intercessions are those in the hospital right now and the rest of the names of the sick are listed in the parish bulletin. My pastoral recommendation is that those who offer the petitions ought to be carefully coached about at least two things. First, there should be a clear separation by means of a pause between the sick and the deceased. We should try as much as possible to avoid any confusion there. Second, as for the names themselves, the ones announcing petitions should be coached about how to pronounce them correctly. When you think about it, having one's name announced among the deceased is the last time that name will be uttered in the liturgy. Names matter.

The concluding prayer is done by the priest. Since the content of the prayer is not specified, the same creativity in composing the petitions would also be encouraged here. But again, here too I would encourage a review of the sample intercessions in the Roman Missal. They are carefully crafted and, from my experience, more succinct than some examples of the Universal Prayer. No prayer can say everything. And the well-known "sobriety" of the Roman Rite can tend to be diluted when this prayer is overly long.

45. Why are the people preparing to become Catholics sent away after the homily? Why can't they stay for the entire Mass?

What you are referring to is an ancient custom that has been revived in the present rites of instructing the catechumenate (the period of up to three years for adults preparing for Christian initiation). From as early as the third century, and certainly strongly attested in the fourth and fifth centuries (in the writings of Saints Augustine, Cyril of Jerusalem, and John Chrysostom), catechumens were "dismissed" from the Sunday Eucharist after the homily. Most often there were prayers for the catechumens and a formula to "dismiss" them. It was only after the catechumens were dismissed that those who remained ("the faithful") joined in the Prayer of the Faithful. The reason catechumens were dismissed was that they were not yet initiated into the church and therefore would not comprehend what was going on at the Eucharist, which action presumed that all present received Communion (which, of course, they could not). Sometimes called the *disciplina arcani*, "the discipline of the secret," this practice also reflected the fact that those not initiated would not know the doctrine or the theological meaning of what occurs in the rest of the Mass. Only after the period of the catechumenate would they know about their faith to the extent that they could participate and know what they were doing at the liturgy. It was at the Easter Vigil that they would share in the rites of the full Eucharist for the first time. That's why for the week after Easter, the newly initiated would return to the bishop and learn all about the sacraments they had received at the vigil. We call these instructions the *mystagogic catecheses*, literally the "instructions on the sacred mysteries."

These historical precedents—and, perhaps more important, the theology behind them—caused the committee that revised the Rites of Christian Initiation for Adults to include the dismissals as a regular feature of the Sunday Mass. Here liturgical tradition grounds our present practice. But this is not to be understood as imitating a historical precedent for its own sake. What I am saying is that if we do this now only because we did it "once upon a time" and "older is better," then we risk delusion and we can appear to avoid the demands of the present. Clearly the "secrecy" factor about the Mass is now absent, given the fact that people can watch the Mass on television regularly or on such special occasions as the liturgy of a papal funeral. So we can't be anachronistic and think that people do not know what is going on at Mass —especially if catechumens have already been coming to Mass for years! But what can become clear is that these dismissals can offer the catechumens (that is, those not baptized) and the candidates for admission into the church (that is, those already baptized in another Christian church) a time to go apart and to reflect more deeply on the Sunday scriptures under the direction of a catechist or teacher. In addition, the very fact of dismissing catechumens and candidates from the Sunday assembly can be a way to reinforce for those who remain who they are as baptized and confirmed members of the church whose privilege it is to share in the Eucharist.

Bottom line: The dismissals are not meant to be penance or a diminishment of who the catechumens and candidates are. They are opportunities for all of us to look forward to their sacramental initiation at Easter, and in the meantime to deepen our appreciation of what the Mass truly is.

VI

Liturgy of the Eucharist

46. Why do we collect actual gifts for the poor at Mass only at Thanksgiving?

The simple answer to your question is *custom*, but it's a custom of a relatively recent vintage. It has really only been since Vatican II that Thanksgiving Day has "caught on" in the United States as a day to celebrate the Eucharist. In fact, in recent years I've heard priests say that this should be a holy day of obligation because it does what holy days originally did in Europe: gather the people for Mass on a holiday. I also suspect that many parishes experience a high level of active participation at Thanksgiving Day Mass because the assembly is an intentional community—people who want to be there and who often share in many of the parish ministries. It is not surprising that on this day of special thanks we would remember the poor and the hungry by collecting actual gifts for them.

Actually, this was among the earliest liturgical traditions of the church—to collect food for the needy as they presented the food to be used for the Eucharist. This custom died out and was replaced by collecting monetary gifts. But again, the origin of this custom was to share our bounty with those in need. The *General Instruction of the Roman Missal* reflects some of these practices when it states that at the "preparation of the gifts...even money or other gifts for the poor or for the Church, brought by the faithful or collected in the church, are acceptable" (n. 73). What is clearly underscored here is the association of eucharistic gifts with serving the poor and needy. Some parishes implement what is envisioned by regularly collecting gifts in the church vestibule, indicating the community's care for the less fortunate.

In addition, the directives for the Evening Mass of the Lord's Supper on Holy Thursday state that "at the beginning of the Liturgy of the Eucharist, there may be a procession of the faithful in which gifts for the poor may be presented with the bread and wine." This is a significant statement because on this most solemn night when we commemorate the institution of the Eucharist, the church asks that we unite our liturgical service with service of the poor. Hence, whether it is on Thanksgiving, on Holy Thursday, on Sundays at the Eucharist, or at other times in connection with gathering for the Eucharist, the link between sharing eucharistic gifts and food for the poor is part of our tradition. This association should be upheld as a key value and concrete expression of what the Mass signifies.

47. Where does the collection money go? And how much should I put into the collection at Mass?

In answering the previous question, I cited the directives of the Missal that indicate that the money is collected for the church and the poor. This suggests that the financial contributions you make go for parish expenses (for example, staff salaries, education expenses, plant maintenance) and designated social justice concerns. With regard to how much you should contribute, I can offer the biblical admonition about tithing and a broader notion of what you might give to the community. In the Bible (see Deut 14:22), the notion of *tithing* means that people were expected to give 10 percent of what they earned from their land. A rather strict interpretation of this injunction applies today in some Christian churches, especially among the Baptists, as opposed to the Catholic custom of giving lesser sums. Part of the reason is that when civil governments oversaw the support of the Catholic faith in parts of Europe, the faithful were relied upon less and less for church support. Their giving habits adjusted accordingly.

In recent years, the Catholic Church in America has sought to frame the discussion of what we give to the church community in terms of stewardship. This means that what we have been given is ours only in the sense that we are free to choose what to do with it for the common good. Part of stewardship is obviously money.

But part of what we have been given for the common good concerns our God-given gifts and talents, which are also to be shared with others. The sound bite "time, talent, treasure" expresses the insight that what we have been given should be shared freely and joyfully with others. One way that some parishes help people explore the ways they can offer their talents is to publicize a range of tasks that can be done by any number of people—for example, education, administration, home visits, legislative advocacy, or liturgical ministry. In this way the limited focus of "how much" in terms of dollars shifts to appreciating that what is *mine* really belongs to *us* and that as a member of the church I am to share what I am and have with others.

But getting back to the original question—how much? A priest-friend of mine advises his parishioners to start with what they receive as an hour's wage. That's the starting point for evaluating what they might consider giving as they work toward the biblical injunction of 10 percent of what I "have" for the Lord.

48. What kind of things should be included in the Offertory Procession? We used to bring up the hosts and water and wine. Now we don't bring up the water. Why?

According to the *General Instruction of the Roman Missal* (n. 73), "it is a praiseworthy practice for the bread and wine to be presented by the faithful....Even money or other gifts for the poor or for the Church, brought by the faithful or collected in the church, are acceptable; given their purpose they are to be put in a suitable place away from the Eucharistic table."

Notice that it states precisely that the eucharistic gifts are "bread and wine" and not water. The rationale here is that these foods are the result of human planting, harvesting, productivity, and manufacture. These are central to our act of self-giving because even though we usually do not bake the eucharistic bread or produce the eucharistic wine as once was customary and expected, nevertheless these gifts reflect the end result of human manufacture and labor, which labor is brought to the liturgy as a sign of our dedication and willingness to give of our talents for the sake of others. An important theological maxim might read "the work of our redemption is enacted in the Mass through the work of human hands."

Behind this act of presenting the bread and wine for the Mass is the liturgical principle that what we consume at Communion should be consecrated at the Mass being celebrated and that only if necessary should we use hosts from the tabernacle for distribution. The historical background here is that, while this was the norm and custom through the Middle Ages, when the laity came to receive Communion less and less, then the emphasis for the Mass to be valid was placed on the priest's receiving Communion from the bread and wine consecrated at that Mass. This was ratified and solidified by the liturgy and teaching of the Council of Trent. As early as the middle of the eighteenth century, however, the popes beginning with Benedict XIV began insisting that all the Communion to be received was consecrated at each Mass. The reason was not just a liturgical nicety. He was concerned that if this did not occur, then the sacrifice of the Mass would be seen as separated from the Communion at Mass, while our theology taught that these were inseparable. Sacrifice and sacrament were one act, which together were essential parts of the Mass. Pope Pius XII reiterated this in modern times. The *General Instruction of the Roman Missal* summarizes this teaching and practice when it says:

> It is most desirable that the faithful, just as the Priest himself is bound to do, receive the Lord's Body from hosts consecrated at the same Mass and that, in the cases where this is foreseen, they partake of the chalice so that even by means of the signs, Communion may stand out more clearly as a participation in the sacrifice actually being celebrated. (n. 85)

49. Is the term *Offertory* still proper to use today? I seem to recall that in the Tridentine Mass the Offertory took much longer and had many more prayers and gestures. What happened?

Your question is very well phrased because you use what was a proper term according to the theology and Mass of Trent. But it isn't any longer. Let me try to explain.

Many of the controversies about the Mass at the time of the Reformation concerned to what extent it was a sacrifice. Debates raged over whether it was or was not, how it could be so, and whether the sacrifice of the Mass repeated or added anything to Christ's sacrifice at Calvary. In light of these disputes, the bishops at the Council of Trent were very clear to state that, yes, the Mass was a sacrifice. A common phrase used after Trent to describe the link between Calvary and the Mass was that the Mass was the "unbloody sacrifice of Calvary." Because the Catholic Church found itself so concerned to emphasize the sacrificial nature of the Mass after Trent, it taught that the three principal parts of the Mass were the Offertory, the Consecration, and the Communion. When these terms were specified, they were interpreted to mean that we offered bread and wine at the Offertory, that at the Consecration they were changed into the body and blood of Christ, and that after the priest received Communion, the sacrament and sacrifice of the Mass was made valid because these three actions had taken place. (And that's why the common understanding in the Tridentine Mass was that you committed no mortal sin if you arrived at Mass in time for the Offertory.)

In the revised Missal, you no longer read about the Offertory at this part of the Mass. In the *General Instruction of the Roman Missal*, it's called the Preparation of the Gifts. In the actual text (of the Ordinary of the Mass) in the Missal, this rite is called the "preparation of the altar and the gifts." This change in terminology signals a change in understanding: the purpose of this rite is to *lead to* the Eucharistic Prayer, not to diminish its prominence in any way, and thus whatever rites are associated with presenting bread and wine should be understood as preparatory for the transformation of the gifts that takes place in the Consecration during the Eucharistic Prayer. You are quite right that in the Tridentine Mass the Offertory was longer and had more ceremony. In fact, the priest raised up the host and the chalice at this point the way he would later do during the Eucharistic Prayer. He also said five prayers that echoed much of the theology of the Roman Canon. The present rite is much more simplified and focuses on placing the gifts on the altar table.

The *General Instruction of the Roman Missal* (n. 72) states that "at the Preparation of the Gifts, bread and wine with water are brought to the altar, the same elements, that is to say, which Christ took into his hands." It then goes on to say:

> It is a praiseworthy practice for the bread and wine to be presented by the faithful. They are then accepted at an appropriate place by the Priest or the Deacon to be carried to the altar. Even though the faithful no longer bring from their own possessions the bread and wine intended for the liturgy as was once the case, nevertheless the rite of carrying up the offerings still keeps its spiritual efficacy and significance. (n. 73)

Hence, what has happened is placing emphasis on both people and priest at this part of the Mass and viewing this rite as a simple transition to the proclamation of the Eucharistic Prayer.

Now, you may ask, is the term *Offertory* or *offering* itself obsolete? Not really. In fact, what has occurred in the present revision of the Mass is that the verb *offer* is found in some form or other in every Eucharistic Prayer. In the Roman Canon, used from the early church through today, it states:

> We, your servants and your holy people,
> offer to your glorious majesty
> from the many gifts you have given us,

> this pure victim,
> this holy victim,
> this spotless victim,
> the holy Bread of eternal life
> and the chalice of everlasting salvation.

This section refers to the consecrated bread and wine, now become the one perfect sacrifice, the very paschal mystery of Christ himself. When we say "we offer" these gifts, we signify that it is the once-offered and unique sacrifice of Christ that we offer to the Father through Christ himself in the unity of the Holy Spirit. The more traditional place for the prayer of "offering" is here at the very section of the Canon (or Eucharistic Prayer) when we commemorate Christ's dying, rising, ascension, and eternal intercession on our behalf at the right hand of God the Father.

In sum: we *present* gifts as we prepare the altar; we *offer* them as Christ himself to the Father in the Eucharistic Prayer.

50. Should the altar really be called the "table"?

In the church's post–Vatican II liturgical writings, it is called both the "altar" and the "table." The *General Instruction of the Roman Missal* states it clearly:

> The altar [*altare*], on which is effected the Sacrifice of the Cross made present under sacramental signs, is also the table of the Lord [*est etiam mensa Domini*] to which the People of God is convoked to participate in the Mass, and it is also the center of the thanksgiving that is accomplished through the Eucharist. (n. 296)

This is a good example of a useful juxtaposition of two emphases whereby the same Eucharist is understood to be both a sacrifice and a holy meal to be shared in. In the revised liturgical documents, most often when the sacrificial nature of the Mass is emphasized, the term *altar* is used and when the communal banquet is emphasized, the term *table* is used. These emphases and terms usually are found together in post–Vatican II literature so that sacrifice and banquet, as well as altar and table, should be understood as inclusive of each other, and not separated.

In the Rite of the Dedication of a Church and an Altar (1977), this same description from the *General Instruction of the Roman Missal* is repeated. But in chapter 4 of the dedication rite, there is also this important sentence: "By instituting in the form of a sacrificial meal the memorial of the sacrifice he was about to offer the Father on the altar of the cross, Christ made holy the table where the community would come to celebrate their Passover" (n. 3). In the following paragraph, the rite states:

> The Christian altar is by its very nature properly the table of sacrifice and of the paschal banquet. It is:
>
> —a unique altar on which the sacrifice of the cross is perpetuated in mystery throughout the ages until Christ comes;
> —a table at which the Church's children come together to give thanks to God and receive the body and blood of Christ. (n. 4)

In Christian antiquity it was common to say that "the altar is Christ." Therefore, it is quite proper that we bow to it as a sign of reverence at the beginning and at the end of Mass.

Part of the difficulty I see today when people ask whether it is an altar or a table is that the rhetoric that is used is often polarizing. It often separates what should not be separated. When some people insist on the sacrificial aspect of the Mass, they are correct in insisting that this emphasis not be lost. But at the same time they should be equally prepared to accept the reemphasis that current church teaching places on the Eucharist as a sacrificial meal. The same is true for some discussions today about the terminology for altar and table. The more we can use both terms, the more faithful we are to church tradition—to all of it, not just that from Trent on—and to the contemporary liturgical directives of the church.

Very little is said about the size or shape of the altar in either the *General Instruction of the Missal* or the rite for its dedication. These texts specify that it should be fixed, that it should be free-standing so that the priest can walk around it, and that the biblical symbolism of its being made of stone should be preserved, although the conference of bishops can permit that it be made of "any becoming, solid, and finely wrought material" (Rite of Dedication, n. 9). Usually the altar is a slight rectangle or a somewhat squared block of solid material. However, nothing in church legislation forbids it from being oblong or rounded. One of my friends, a Maryknoll Missioner stationed in Hong Kong, was responsible for constructing a new church and parish center in the suburbs of the center of the city. Because the Chinese customarily eat at round tables, he designed the altar in an oblong shape precisely to underscore the fact that the Mass is a communal meal. I also suspect that part of his motivation was to capitalize on the emphasis that the Chinese culture places on the act of dining together. This cultural assumption of dining together would be most helpful not only in explaining the nature of the Mass but also to describe the very nature of Christianity—as a religion of communal faith and shared identity. This in itself could be quite a countercultural reality in the face of the kind of individualism that marks much of the theology and practice of Eastern religions. For one to become a convert to Christianity in general, and to the sacramental system of Catholicism in particular, requires quite a shift in outlook about what religion is all about in the first place. Obviously, for my priest-friend the symbolic link with familial dining at a round table for daily food served as a significant symbolic precedent to interpret the theology of the Mass as well as the nature of the Christian church and its theology.

51. Why does the church through the whole world have to use bread and wine for Mass?

The short answer to your question is that we do what Jesus did. The more appropriate answer brings up three questions of its own: Why did Jesus do what he did? What do bread and wine signify? And what does custom have to do with this?

Why did Jesus use bread and wine? The scriptures repeatedly tell us that he was an observant Jew. In his role as a rabbi and teacher, he would follow Jewish custom and host his disciples to a weekly Sabbath meal or, in the case of the Last Supper, he was host at a meal with strong Passover overtones. The memorial meal of the Jews commemorated their liberation from bondage in Egypt. They told the story of their being freed and shared in the banquet commemorating it, which meal included bread and wine—the staples of the Middle Eastern diet to this day. These foods were the means Jesus used to commemorate his coming passing over from death to new life. His act of blessing bread and wine at the Last Supper involved a solemn declaration that from now on it was his Passover the disciples would commemorate and their/our unity through and with him to new life. The command "Do this in memory of me" is the basis for our engaging in this same kind of blessing prayer at Mass, words spoken over bread and wine. The bread and wine of Judaism's sacred meals became the food of Christianity's sacred meal, the Eucharist.

What does bread and wine signify? As I hinted in answering the question about what is proper to bring up at the Presentation of the Gifts at Mass (question 48), the symbols of bread and wine are very significant because they are the result of human manufacture. That means that the process that we humans engage in in order to produce these foodstuffs has many levels of meaning and we need to look at the process and the result to appreciate why we still use bread and wine at Mass. The baking of bread involves a series of actions that themselves are regarded as *paschal*, meaning dying and rising. (The same is true for wine. But for brevity we'll discuss bread and make an application to wine at the end.) The beginning of the process is planting and harvesting. In at least a metaphorical sense, the grain of wheat first has to die (John 12:24) to yield rich fruit. Seed has to be planted in the ground to produce the shafts of wheat, which are themselves cut down, harvested, then milled into flour. Hence, even the flour itself has a paschal symbolism. Then the baking of bread requires kneading and (normally) a series of risings before it is baked and fresh bread is produced. Again, the process of baking itself also sustains a level of paschal symbolism. The same is true for wine: planting, harvesting grapes, crushing them into liquid, fermentation, all involved in the "paschal" process of making the wine. My point is that these foods themselves are central symbols of paschal dying and rising and hence are most fitting to represent the Eucharist as our sharing in Christ, our food for eternal life.

Finally, a word about custom: It was because bread and wine were the customary foods for Jewish ceremonial meals that Jesus used them and we follow this precedent. But it was also customary through the early Middle Ages that Christians used leavened bread at the Eucharist. And to this day it is still customary to use leavened bread in the Eastern churches for the Eucharist. The reason why the West came to use only unleavened bread was that, as fewer and fewer people actually received Communion at Mass and as concern grew to revere the eucharistic elements, it was judged best to use unleavened bread because there would be fewer crumbs that might inadvertently not be eaten and therefore reverently received. The fact that the East uses leavened bread and the West uses unleavened bread indicates a certain variety in the use of bread and represents diversity in unity. But the fact that we all use bread and wine is to be true to what Jesus did.

52. When should the priest go to the altar and when should he leave it?

As I begin to respond to your question I am thinking of the familiar mantra of realtors when it comes to assessing the value of a property: "Location, location, location." This came to mind because where and how individual parts of the Mass take place offers much to reflect on theologically. Up to now I am sure you have noticed that I have continually referred to what the liturgy says in explaining what the Mass is. Your question invites us to realize that the location of *where* we do different parts of the Mass can often tell us something very important about that part of the Mass. In effect, the locations are at the altar, the chair, and the ambo.

At the beginning and at the end of Mass, the priest (and deacon) reverence the altar, normally by kissing it. The priest then goes to the chair from which he presides over the Liturgy of the Word. He moves to the ambo to proclaim the gospel and to deliver the homily from there, or from the chair or other suitable place. The Missal then states that the priest moves to stand at the altar in order to place the bread and wine on it during the Presentation of the Gifts, and he leaves the altar to distribute Communion. After the distribution he "may return to the chair." After a period of silence, he says the Prayer after Communion "standing at the chair or the altar."

By way of contrast, in the extraordinary form of the low Mass, the priest stays at the altar for the whole Mass. At a solemn Mass he moves from the bench to the altar several times during the Mass. The reason why this was stipulated in the solemn Tridentine Mass and is required for every Mass is that, like all other liturgy, the Mass involves movement, processions, and gestures. It also emphasizes three principal locations as receiving emphasis during the Mass: the chair, the ambo, and the altar itself. These three locations emphasize different aspects of the Mass, especially the location for proclaiming the Word at the lectern and for the proclamation of the Eucharistic Prayer at the altar.

53. Sometimes the priest says prayers over the bread and wine, and we respond, "Blessed be God forever," but sometimes he doesn't. Why?

Well, as I mentioned in answer to question 49 about the Offertory, one of clearest examples of revising the Mass was the decision after Vatican II to reduce severely the number and kind of prayers said over the bread and wine as they are placed on the altar. The committee charged with the task of revising the Mass simply took out all the prayers in the 1962 Missal. But since this was

thought to be too drastic a change, the decision was made to introduce the (briefer) texts you refer to. Technically these aren't prayers
because prayers name and address God, name our need, and ask
that it be granted through Christ—and at the end, we all say,
"Amen." The texts at the Presentation of the Gifts are acclamations
acknowledging God's rule over all creation, our participation in
manufacturing the bread and wine, and the concluding acclamation "Blessed be God forever." Now some have questioned the
legitimacy of these acclamations because their origin is the same
genre of Jewish prayers that is the basis for the Eucharistic Prayer
itself. In fact, I'd even go so far as to say that the very problem that
those who reformed the Missal wanted to change (because the
prayers at the Offertory resembled the Roman Canon) in effect
produced the same result as before, since both the Eucharistic
Prayer and these presentation texts are from the same matrix of
Jewish prayer!

The directions in the Missal now state that the priest takes
the bread, "holding it slightly raised above the altar" (in a gesture
that shows the bread to the people, not in an elaborate gesture of
offering as at the Final Doxology and Great Amen), and "says in a
low voice" the "Blessed are you, Lord God of all creation" text. So
from the outset we learn that these texts are not meant to be heard
by the gathered assembly. Hence, the issue you raise in your question concerns when you hear the prayers said aloud and when you
do not. But then the Missal states, "If, however, the Offertory
Chant is not sung, the Priest may speak these words aloud; at the
end the people may acclaim, 'Blessed be God forever.'" Notice the
careful use of the word *may*, which again signifies that these prayers
are considered relatively unimportant, especially as compared with
the other prayers of the Mass: the presidential prayers, and especially the Eucharistic Prayer itself. The other thing to note is that
the Missal is filled with directions about how the priest should celebrate the Mass and that not all prayers are to be said aloud. The
fact that we hear these texts over the bread and wine as often as we
do may indicate that we need to be more attentive to what the

Missal actually says. When you say and hear every text in the Missal, the result may be that the more important texts seem like all the others. There are gradations to the Mass prayers. The texts at the Presentation of the Gifts are clearly less, not more important than others. The very use of the term *may* means there is an option. Perhaps part of the reason is because "less is more"!

54. Why does the priest wash his hands at Mass? They certainly don't seem to be dirty.

The historical background to this rite comes (once again) from the Jewish Passover ritual. At the time when the father of the family was about to break the blessed bread and distribute it to the gathered family and friends, he would wash his hands as a sign of purification. Hence, there is a spiritual, ritual background to what was also a custom in the Roman Rite.

If you recall my answer to question 46, I stated that the earliest descriptions we have of the Presentation of the Gifts at Mass include all kinds of foodstuffs, in addition to bread and wine. These foods, such as wine, cheese, oil, and fresh fruits and vegetables, were brought forward at Mass so that afterward they could be distributed to the poor. (Deacons most usually did this.) You and I know what happens to our hands when we choose foods at the market and unpack those foods when we get home. So you can well imagine that the priest needed to wash his hands before handling the eucharistic gifts at the altar and at Communion. Another reason why the priest may have had to wash his hands was after he used incense over the eucharistic gifts. Still to this day when the priest uses incense at Mass, his hands may get dirty because of the charcoal and smoke. Hence, the custom of washing hands had another practical meaning.

But because these practices died out (or were rarely engaged in) and also because of the sacred nature of what the priest is about to do when he prays the Eucharistic Prayer and consecrates the bread and wine to become the body and blood of Christ, the ritual of washing hands took on greater symbolic, spiritual value. It became a sign of interior purification and integrity of heart. Some scholars argue that the spiritual meaning came to be attached to hand washing in parts of Europe and eventually came to be the practice in Rome. In any event it is still part of the Mass, and in the revised Missal when he washes his hands, the priest says inaudibly one verse from Psalm 51:4:

> Wash me, O Lord, from my iniquity
> And cleanse me from my sin.

55. At the Preparation of the Gifts, the priest says, "Pray...that *my* sacrifice and *yours* may be acceptable to God the almighty Father." But at other places the priest refers to "*our* sacrifice." What does this mean?

Your question raises a number of important liturgical and theological issues, starting with the meaning of what the priest does at Mass when he uses plural pronouns such as *we, our,* and *us.* I tell my students that the trick to understanding the Mass is the pronouns and the way that the prayers almost always use the plural form, even when one person, the priest or deacon, is praying them. I'd say that 99 percent of the pronouns in the Mass prayers are plural. Classically this indicates that the Mass is always a communal action of the whole church and that even when individual persons pray, they speak for and with the whole community. Therefore, the major prayers of the Mass—for example, the presidential prayers of the priest (the Collect, Prayer over the Gifts, Eucharistic Prayer, Prayer after Communion) and almost all of the responses of the people—use the communal *we,* as in "We ask this through Christ our Lord." On a more technical level, the phrase that the church uses to describe how and why it is that the priest prays for the whole church is "in the person of the church" (*in persona ecclesiae*), which means that the prayer of the priest is always done on behalf of the whole church.

In the present Missal, the most obvious places where *I* is used
is in the Creed (because it is a reiteration of our baptismal faith) and
at the invitation to Communion when we echo the words of the
centurion in the Gospel of Matthew (8:8): "I am not worthy that
you should enter under my roof." We retain the *I* form precisely
because this is a quote from the scriptures. Then there are the cases
when the priest uses the *I* and *my* form—during prayers of personal
devotion not meant to be said aloud (and therefore not heard by the
gathered assembly). For the priest, this occurs in the words he prays
to himself at his Communion: "Free me by this, your most holy
Body and Blood, from all my sins…." This prayer originated in the
ninth century and was added to the liturgy as a prayer to remind the
priest of his personal unworthiness. Hence, the statements "I confess" (which was originally a prayer of the priest and the server, not
of the people) and the prayer "Free me by this, your most holy Body
and Blood…" before his Communion came to be parts of the Mass,
though always regarded as less important theologically than the
prayers I referred to above (for example, presidential prayers). The
rationale here is that the priest had to declare his unworthiness and
he did so during Mass. But these were regarded as private prayers and
were not to be confused with the public prayers, true to the nature
of the liturgy, which are normally in the communal *we* form.

Now back to your precise question. The part of the Mass you
are referring to is called the "invitation to prayer" and contains an
explicit invitation by the priest: "Pray, brethren, that my sacrifice
and yours (Latin, *meum ac vestrum*, literally "mine and yours") may
be acceptable…" The people respond, "May the Lord accept the
sacrifice at your hands" (*de manibus tuis*, literally "from your
hands"). In the extraordinary form of the Mass, this series of texts
was originally done apart from the assembly's hearing. The priest
said, "*Orate fratres…* ("Pray, brethren"), to which the server made
the reply. This meant that this part of the Mass was in effect totally
silent as far as the congregation was concerned. In addition, historical research indicates that the origins of this dialogue may well
have been from the eighth century when here the priest addressed

other ministers in the sanctuary in a low voice. Again it would have been done, in effect, in silence. But what was approaching was the most important part of the Mass, the Consecration during the Eucharistic Prayer. Hence, in the Middle Ages it was decided to have the first part of this dialogue spoken aloud by the priest (who turned and faced the people at this point) to indicate the importance of what was to follow and to invite the congregation's attention. The phrasing, which used the singular pronoun form ("my sacrifice and yours"), reflected the emphasis on the Eucharist as a central experience of an individual's salvation. But at the same time it is important to realize that no other classical prayers of the Mass were changed to fit this theology. For example, the text of the Roman Canon repeatedly asserts the plural: "To you…most merciful Father, we make humble prayer and petition."

56. The Prayer over the Gifts was once called the "Secret." Can you explain?

This is another case where terminology developed because of what occurred liturgically. The earliest evidence we have of a prayer at this part of the Mass calls it the Prayer over the Gifts, principally because after the gifts were collected and the bread and wine were placed on the altar, there was one "collect" type of prayer that the priest said over them. Sometimes this prayer referred to what the church community desired as a result of their participation in the Mass. Therefore, petitions for peace, unity, forgiveness of sins, and so on, were common. At other times these prayers referred to what these gifts were as signs of our devotion to God. At still other times these prayers linked the particular feast being celebrated with the eucharistic action, for example, the sacrifice that a martyr offered in giving his or her life as that act reflected Christ's self-sacrifice as perpetuated in the Mass.

During the Middle Ages, for a variety of reasons, what was always regarded as the high point of the Mass, the proclamation of the Eucharistic Prayer, came to be regarded as the priest's solemn prayer, which he spoke in a very soft voice. This led to an emphasis on the "silent Canon" as being very fitting because silence could be taken for reverence and something very sacred. Now what happened to the Prayer over the Gifts was that it too came to be prayed almost silently. The reason was that it was so close to the Canon and if the Canon was silent and so sacred, it was a logical step to view this prayer as a silent introduction to the silent Canon. Hence, the way it was prayed—softly, or perhaps "secretly"—was the principal reason it came to be called the "secret."

57. Why are there three parts to the introduction to the Preface and the Eucharistic Prayer?

Your question allows me to say a little more about the importance of the Eucharistic Prayer at Mass, much of which I have been hinting at all along. The *General Instruction of the Roman Missal* (n. 78) states that the Eucharistic Prayer is the "center and high point of the entire celebration." This insight is reflected in the way the prayer is introduced, namely, the three-part dialogue you are referring to. Where does this come from? Its origins are from the Jewish custom whereby an introduction, such as "the Lord be with you," would signal that an important proclamation was to follow. In Christianity, as early as the third-century liturgical rites found in the *Apostolic Tradition* of Hippolytus of Rome, the same three phrases we use today were found in the introduction to the Eucharistic Prayer. "The Lord be with you" specifies what is already occurring in the Mass, that the Lord is indeed with us. Also, as a greeting, it engages our attention and reminds us of what is occurring throughout the Mass and that the proclamation of the Eucharistic Prayer will contain a special, lyrical summary of God's mighty deeds on our behalf through salvation history. "Lift up your hearts" invites us to be especially attentive to what is to follow, not just with minds and intellectual faculties, but with our hearts—in other words, with our whole selves. The last part, "Let us give thanks to the Lord our God," specifies exactly what is to follow: our offer of praise and thanks to God for creation and redemption. Our response here that "it is right and just" comes from Roman legal rhetoric, which would commonly use the phrase *right and just* to signify a willing-ness to do what is in one's competence and what one should feel responsible for. The importance of this phrase is seen in the fact that it is repeated in the next line from the priest—"It is truly right and just"—and forms something of an echo of our response. This is to say that the first words the priest says in the Preface are, literally, "It is truly right and just" (the same Latin phrase we just used, plus the intensive formed with the word *vere,* or "truly") "that we should always and everywhere give you thanks."

What should be clear is that this introduction sets up and emphasizes the Eucharistic Prayer, that its phrasing is not arbitrary, and that its threefold structure indicates the high value placed on the Eucharistic Prayer that follows.

58. What does the term *Preface* mean in relation to the other term *Eucharistic Prayer?*

Your question asks for both a theological and a historical response. Theologically the Preface is part of the Eucharistic Prayer. We are accustomed to using the term *preface* to refer to an introduction, but in the Mass the meaning of *preface* comes from the prefix *pre-*, which refers to the fact that this text is prayer "before God" and "before the congregation," meaning that what follows is proclaimed and stated before others.

What caused the separation between the Preface and the Eucharistic Prayer offers another instance of why it is important to understand the historical evolution of the Mass. From the fifth century up until Vatican II, the Roman Rite had one Eucharistic Prayer, the Roman Canon. It was called *Roman* because of its ori-gins as from the "Roman" tradition, the rites associated with Rome. It was called the *Canon,* from the Latin term meaning "fixed," because it was used daily and no other text replaced it. But before we go out too far on a limb, let me also say that the Roman Canon, while a fixed structure, also contained sections within it that changed for a given liturgical feast or season. This practice characterizes the present Missal, which has parts of the Canon for

Christmas, Easter, and so on. Given this structure, it is not a surprise that the first part of the Canon, which had the greatest number of variable texts, came to be called the Preface because this text
changed almost daily, and it led to the more fixed Canon that followed. In the earliest collection of Missal prayers we have (called
the Verona manuscript or the Leonine Sacramentary), we find over
two hundred and sixty prefaces! This number diminished over time
with the result that the extraordinary form of the Mass contains a
dozen (as I noted in answer to question 23). The present reform
sought to offer much greater variety in the prefaces and eucharistic prayers (see questions 60 and 61). Today we have over ninety
prefaces in the Missal. It may not be the number the Leonine
Sacramentary boasted, but it is clearly an important attribute of the
present Missal. Theologically and liturgically today it is best to
understand that the Preface and the Eucharistic Prayer go together
and are intrinsically connected.

59. Sometimes we sing the "Holy, Holy, Holy" and other parts of the Eucharistic Prayer, and sometimes we don't sing them. Why? How important are these acclamations?

Your question is an important one, especially because it indicates how the Eucharistic Prayer is not a monologue by the priest.
In the earliest description of the structure of the Mass, which we
have from the *First Apology* of Justin the Martyr (150), at the end
of the Eucharistic Prayer the people sang "Amen." This conclusion
was said to be resounding and a very significant affirmation of "so
be it" by the whole assembly. Then by the time we have textual
evidence of the Roman Canon (fifth century), we find the "Holy,
Holy, Holy" acclamation you are referring to. It was originally sung
by all present and was called the *Sanctus* because it began with a
threefold *Sanctus, sanctus, sanctus.* However, by the time the Canon
came to be silent, it was said by the server(s) and the priest himself
at the low Mass, but in a very soft voice. (As with most of their

involvement in the Mass, the servers functioned as a substitute for the whole congregation.) In the extraordinary form of the high and solemn Mass, it is always sung, sometimes by the choir or schola but oftentimes by the whole congregation.

One of the main features of the present Missal has been the restoration of the Eucharistic Prayer to central prominence by having the priest proclaim it aloud (or sing it) and by having the whole assembly join in three specific acclamations during it. These acclamations are the *Sanctus* (Holy, Holy, Holy), the Mystery of Faith (one of three choices), and the final Amen, sometimes called the Great Amen. The *General Instruction of the Roman Missal* states that "the whole congregation, joining with the heavenly powers, sings the *Sanctus* ('Holy, holy, holy'). This acclamation, which constitutes part of the Eucharistic Prayer itself, is pronounced by all the people with the Priest" (n. 78 b).

Recall what I said in the answer to question 57, namely, that the Eucharistic Prayer is a solemn declaration of praise and thanks for God's gifts to us of creation and redemption. Now recall the text of the *Sanctus* acclamation. The first part acclaims God because "heaven and earth are full of [his] glory." This first part of this text is adapted from Isaiah 6:2–3, which was a common feature of Jewish liturgical prayer, especially at the synagogue service of the word at morning prayer. It is a lyrical prayer that praises God for the gift of creation. This is a central feature of Jewish liturgical prayer and our Christian liturgical experience. It is important that we not forget that we revere and acclaim a God of both creation and redemption. The second part of the acclamation, "Blessed is he who comes in the name of the Lord," is from Matthew 21:9. It serves as a link to this second motif of the Eucharistic Prayer— praising God for redemption. In some eucharistic prayers in history, the praise for God's outstretched hand of redemption to Israel is summarized here; in the present Missal, this theme is very clear in Eucharistic Prayer IV. In all eucharistic prayers, God is then praised and thanked for Christ's gracious act of redemption and all that he did for our sakes and for our salvation.

The acclamation called the Mystery of Faith—which follows the words of institution ("this is my body...this is my blood")—is new to the Mass since Vatican II and is not in the extraordinary form of the Mass. The rationale here is that if the Mass is essentially the actualization of Christ's paschal mystery as *the* mystery of faith, it would make sense to emphasize this part of the Eucharistic Prayer with an acclamation—hence the "invention" of the acclamation the Mystery of Faith. We now have three choices for the text of this acclamation, each of which specifies Christ's death and resurrection, and two of which explicitly mention the second coming. The Mystery of Faith is therefore a most useful expression for the assembly to use to make the Eucharistic Prayer its own, as well as ratify in song what is occurring through the priest's proclamation and action. The Final Doxology at the end of the Eucharistic Prayer ("through him, with him...") concludes with the people's assent, the affirmation "Amen," meaning "so be it." This is the acclamation that Justin asserted was done robustly!

Hence, we can say that the acclamations are the "people's parts" of the Eucharistic Prayer and should be sung or said by all present. In the Tridentine Mass, the *Sanctus* and Amen were sung by the choir largely because the choir had taken over almost all of the spoken and sung means of participating in the Mass. In the present use of the extraordinary form they can be sung by the whole gathered assembly. I would suggest that they should be sung by everyone, given the emphasis they receive in the *General Instruction of the Roman Missal* (n. 40). In the document *Sing to the Lord*, the American bishops state that

> the people take part in the Eucharistic Prayer by listening attentively to the words sung or spoken by the priest and joining their hearts and minds to the actions of the prayer. Their voices should be joined together in the acclamations of the Eucharistic Prayer, including the Sanctus, the great cosmic acclamation of praise; the Memorial Acclamation [now referred to as the Mystery of Faith], by

which the faithful participate in keeping the memory of Christ's Paschal Mystery; and the Amen that follows the concluding doxology, by which they give their assent to the entire prayer. These acclamations should be sung, especially on Sundays and solemnities. (n. 180)

The fact that you don't always sing them, but that you say them, probably indicates that this occurs at Masses when there is no music at all. This is understandable given where we have been with liturgical music after Trent. But I need to be true to all of the official instructions about music in the reformed liturgy by asserting once more that the singing of these acclamations is meant to be part of every Mass. In terms of the theology of the Mass, they deserve this emphasis because the *Sanctus* summarizes the themes of the Eucharistic Prayer, the Mystery of Faith is the people's ratification and affirmation that this prayer also enacts Christ's paschal mystery, and the Amen is our solemn assent to what has taken place in this prayer.

60. Why did we have one Canon in the Tridentine Mass, and now we have ten of them in the Mass after Vatican II?

First let me begin by adjusting your terminology in light of my answer to question 58. Technically, the term *Roman Canon* refers to the "fixed" text of the Eucharistic Prayer (*canon* means "fixed") that has been in use in the Catholic Church since the fifth century. Also technically, the term does not refer to the other eucharistic prayers now in use. But, at the risk of sounding like a logic class professor, I need to say that all the other prayers, as well as the Canon, are called eucharistic prayers precisely because they are prayers of "thanks and praise" (*Eucharist* means "thanksgiving").

Why do we have additional texts now? One of the most important persons who influenced this particular change in the Mass was Father Cipriano Vagaggini. His book *The Canon of the Mass and Liturgical Reform* describes the rationale for this change. In the first part of the book, he summarizes many of the strengths of the Roman Canon: its emphasis on Christ, its emphasis on the apostles and saints of the Catholic Church, its emphasis on intercession, its emphasis on what we gain from joining in the Mass, and so on. But then he goes on to evaluate the single Roman Canon in light of the wealth of other eucharistic prayers that liturgical history has given us from other rites. Here he notes, among other things, the almost complete lack of any mention of the Holy Spirit in the Canon, its (perhaps) overemphasis on intercession, and the fact that the Roman Rite's precedent for variety in the prefaces could well substantiate a move toward adding new eucharistic prayers to the Mass—for the sake of variety especially if it is a prayer that will be proclaimed in the vernacular. These suggestions were taken very seriously and the result was to make some slight editing adjustments to the Canon and to add three "new" eucharistic prayers to the Missal.

I put *new* in quotes because all of these are really not new compositions. For example, what we now call Eucharistic Prayer II is actually adapted and edited from that same document I quoted in answer to question 57, the *Apostolic Tradition* of Hippolytus of Rome. This text was offered as a model for a newly ordained bishop to use at his ordination Eucharist. The text as we have it in the Missal has been adjusted and the *Sanctus* acclamation has been added. But its origin and base is from the third century in Rome. Eucharistic Prayer III was put together by Father Vagaggini himself from some material from North Africa. Eucharistic Prayer IV is certainly the longest and most embellished theologically. Its source is the Eastern liturgical tradition, and its most important influence is from the *Apostolic Constitutions* from Antioch. This prayer has its own preface, which cannot be substituted for by any other preface. The reason? The next time you hear it at Mass you will notice that the praise of God for creation is the dominant theme of the Preface, which motif continues in the first part of the Eucharistic Prayer that follows the *Sanctus*. Since all the other prefaces acclaim and describe facets of Christ's redemption as motives for praising God, if we were to use any one of them this theology would jar with the next part of Eucharistic Prayer IV about creation and God's covenant relationship with Israel ("Time and time again you offered them covenants").

That gives us four. Then what happened? After the publication of the *Directory for Masses with Children* (1973), it was judged useful to compose eucharistic prayers that would be more suitable for children's comprehension. This led to the publication of three eucharistic prayers for children. A chief feature of these three prayers is that in addition to the three eucharistic acclamations of the Mystery of Faith that we just talked about in answer to question 59, shorter acclamations were added, interspersed throughout the prayer as a way of keeping the children focused on the eucharistic action by singing them. In the first of the eucharistic prayers for Masses with children, this acclamation separates the two sections of the *Sanctus*, makes them into two acclamations, then the entire *Sanctus* is sung at the usual place. In the second and third of these prayers, single-line acclamations run throughout the prayer: "Glory to God in the highest," "Hosannah in the highest," "Jesus has given his life for us," and "We praise you, we bless you, we thank you."

Then, in preparation for the holy year of renewal and reconciliation in 1975, Pope Paul VI asked that two additional prayers be prepared on the theme of reconciliation. Now in the interests of "full disclosure," I should point out that there was some debate at that time about whether there should be additional eucharistic prayers. The argument against adding prayers was that we should allow the seven prayers then in use to be appropriated and assimilated fully since, after all, this was the first time the Roman Church had any prayers other than the single Roman Canon. In addition, the sense was that the Eucharistic Prayer should become so well known that people would welcome its familiar cadences, phrases, and images. Pope Paul VI, without negating any of this reasoning, still judged that the holy year theme of renewal and reconciliation was so important—and so intrinsic to the church's life—that the addition of two prayers was warranted. They were published in vernacular languages in six months.

The most recent prayer to be added to the Missal originally came from Switzerland. It was composed as a prayer to be used in that county to prepare for a national meeting (called the Swiss Synod). Then it was translated into Italian and used for over a decade in Italy. The American bishops received permission from Rome to use it as part of our Missal. It has the (rather awkward) title "Eucharistic Prayer for Masses for Various Needs and Occasions." The text is really a collection of separate parts of a prayer, with four prefaces (entitled "The Church on the Way to Unity," "God Guides the Church on the Way to Salvation," "Jesus, the Way to the Father," and "Jesus, the Compassion of God"). The Missal states that the priest chooses one of these prefaces and then chooses the intercessory prayer in the Eucharistic Prayer that corresponds to the theme of the preface.

This variety and flexibility reflects the origins and present text of the Roman Canon—"fixed" in the sense of the same structure but varying parts within it.

61. Somehow the new Eucharistic Prayer sounds different from the Roman Canon. In fact, I almost never hear the Roman Canon anymore. Can you explain this?

Let me answer your second question first because it leads to why new eucharistic prayers were added after Vatican II. In his work on *The Canon of the Mass and Liturgical Reform*, Father Cipriano Vagaggini noted that a "possible defect" of the Roman Canon was its lack of a cohesive structure and unity of ideas. (I say *possible defect* because I do not want to seem to judge out of hand a prayer that has lasted the test of time and was used throughout the Roman Church from the fifth to the twentieth century!) But the fact that it is a collection of variable parts had the downside of seeming to be a less-than-cohesive prayer, especially when compared with eucharistic prayers from other sources, particularly Eastern ones. I suspect that this lack of cohesion in the Canon, especially when compared with the three new additional eucharistic prayers, is the reason why priests more usually choose the new texts. What I would like to suggest, however, is that the Canon be used especially on the special feasts when specific parts of the prayer are included for that day, for example, Christmas, Epiphany, Easter, and so on.

Now to the broader question of the differences between the Canon and the new prayers. The "story behind the story" of the need for new prayers (documented amply in Father Vagaggini's book, largely because he was in charge of the committee that did this work) is that liturgical scholars in the past century discovered a wealth of eucharistic prayers that have been used over the course of centuries, especially in the Eastern churches. What this did was enable scholars to study manuscripts and collections of texts and to see that, in fact, the Eucharistic Prayer could have some different or additional elements from those found in the Roman Canon. Because of this textual evidence of variety, the study group charged with adapting the Canon and adding prayers set about its work on the basis of sound historical discoveries and scientific methods. Now back to your question. Yes, the structure of the new texts is different. But the facts that at least one of the new eucharistic prayers (Eucharistic Prayer II) is shorter than the Canon, that they have a logical structure, and that they clearly emphasize the role of the Holy Spirit make them certainly worthy of frequent use. Let me outline this structure and make some comments on it.

According to the *General Instruction of the Roman Missal*, the chief elements that make up the Eucharistic Prayer are thanksgiving, acclamation, Epiclesis, institution, anamnesis, offering, intercessions, and Final Doxology (n. 79). "Thanksgiving" refers to the nature of the prayer as a solemn declaration of praise and thanks. It is especially prominent in the Preface where a specific aspect of God's work of salvation is noted. For example, Preface 1 of Easter states: "By dying he has destroyed our death, and by rising restored our life." Thus at Easter we praise God for Christ's paschal mystery and our becoming sharers in it, especially as this participation is renewed in the liturgy. (There is a whole catechesis on why the liturgy matters in this last sentence. Notice the pronouns!) The second element, "acclamation," refers to the church's joining the praise of the "angels and saints" as we sing "Holy, holy, holy," as well as to the Mystery of Faith after the words of institution and the Great Amen after the Final Doxology. (Recall my response to question 59.)

For us in the Roman Catholic Church, the next element of the prayer is new—the Epiclesis. This is the element that Father Vagaggini did not find in the Canon, and its restoration was judged to be necessary. The Epiclesis refers to an explicit invocation that God, through the power of the Holy Spirit, consecrate the gifts we present at the Eucharist, and that the church may become more unified as a result of this invocation and eucharistic celebration. In the text of most eucharistic prayers in liturgical history, this prayer explicitly invokes the power of the Holy Spirit, but there are instances when it is an invocation of Christ (under the term *Logos*). Therefore, in the second Eucharistic Prayer we find the words:

> Make holy, therefore, these gifts, we pray,
> by sending down your Spirit upon them like the dewfall,
> so that they may become for us
> the Body and Blood of our Lord Jesus Christ.

The other theme of the Epiclesis prayer is for the church's unity. Hence, in that same prayer we have the text:

> Humbly we pray
> that, partaking of the Body and Blood of Christ,
> we may be gathered into one by the Holy Spirit.

These two themes—transformation of the gifts and the unity of the church—are classic in the liturgical tradition of the churches, are specific to the Epiclesis, and reflect the crucial role that the Holy Spirit plays in the action of the Eucharist. Hence, these parts of every Eucharistic Prayer added to the Mass are an extremely important addition to our prayer.

The next element of the Eucharistic Prayer is the "institution narrative and consecration." As I am sure you have noticed, when the priest gets to this part of all the Eucharistic Prayers, he begins to use the words of Jesus from the Last Supper: "Take this, all of you...this is my body...blood." In the structure of the Eucharistic Prayer, these words take on an even greater significance as the wider framework of the Last Supper is recalled. Our attention is thus drawn to the wider canvas and not just to the text "this is my body...blood." The fact that this section is called the "institution narrative and consecration" signals an emphasis on the words and gestures that recall the Last Supper when Jesus instituted this sacramental action.

The next element, with the name *anamnesis*, needs a bit of background to understand. Literally this term is a transliteration of the Greek word for "memorial." But the kind of memorial indicated here comes from the Jewish and scriptural understanding of what *memorial* means. For the Jew of Jesus' day (and to our own times), the notion of remembrance is not merely a mental exercise. Rather, *memorial* means that we invoke God's action and presence and ask that it be active among us now. A saying of the rabbis— "To remember is to give life, to forget is to let die"—is a good way of appreciating what anamnesis means. When we engage in a prayer of remembrance, God does something for us. When we ask God to "forget" something, like sin, then it has no existence. You can see, therefore, how important this part of the Eucharistic Prayer is, especially the command "do this in memory of me." We come to Mass to *do* what Jesus commanded. We don't just come to think about the way it was in Palestine in his lifetime. Rather, what we are doing is commemorating—literally "remembering together"— what God has done through Christ, and in the remembering, experiencing it as fully and deeply as is humanly possible. It makes sense, therefore, that the church would want to emphasize this part of the prayer with the new Mystery of Faith acclamation (which normally precedes this part of the prayer, but which in the eucharistic prayers for Masses with children follows the memorial prayer itself).

The next section, the "offering," explicitates what we do in the Mass—we offer Christ to the Father and at the same time we surrender ourselves to God through, with, and in Christ. *This* is the classic place where the language of *offer* and *offering* is found in the Mass, not at what we used to call the Offertory. (For more on this, see question 49). The next section, the "intercessions," was admittedly a chief feature of the Roman Canon. What happened in the revision of the Missal and the addition of the new eucharistic prayers is that these intercessions are set within a larger prayer with several other themes. This means that while we do admit and name what we ask God for in the Mass, we don't make this so central that other aspects of the prayer are diminished, especially praise and thanks for the mighty acts of salvation. The dynamic in this prayer (as well as in all liturgical prayer) is a balance between praise and petition, a balance between thanks and request.

The Final Doxology concludes these prayers. This is a very important example of the relationship of the church to the Trinity. In the Final Doxology we assert that all we have done is through, with, and in Christ. We also assert that all that we do in the Mass—especially offering our praise and thanks—is "in the unity of the Holy Spirit." Now this phrase deserves some unpacking! On one level, the more obvious one, this phrase refers to the Holy Spirit, the third person of the Trinity. But on another, less obvious but nonetheless very important level, this phrase refers to the community that makes up the church. You see, according to the famous liturgical scholar Josef Jungmann, "in the unity of the Holy Spirit" refers to the members of the church that, in their coming together in unity, make up the praying church at the Eucharist. Hence, at the end of the Eucharistic Prayer what we have is a very fitting combination of factors that really summarize what the Eucharistic Prayer is all about: naming the persons of the Trinity and naming the church as the community of believers that gathers for this unique act of offering thanks and praise as we remember Christ's paschal death and resurrection.

I'm sure you can now see why you have a different sense when you hear the new eucharistic prayers that mirror this outline most concretely. To help you get even more out of this part of the Mass, I suggest that you read over and meditate on the texts of the eucharistic prayers. The more we know the logical flow and the wording of what we pray at this part of the Mass, the more it will become what it is meant to be: "the center and summit of the entire celebration" (*General Instruction*, n. 78).

62. I don't hear a lot about the Consecration. I was taught that it was the most important part of the Mass. What happened?

For anyone who was accustomed to participating in the Mass before Vatican II, your question resonates very well. Indeed we were taught that the Consecration was the most important part of the Mass. This was because of the Reformation controversies and our need to insist that our theology and practice of the Eucharist emphasized the real presence of Christ as much as possible. (For example, the mandatory ringing of bells at this point in the Mass.) Now that those pressures have lifted, we have come to appreciate other aspects of the Mass as also important, such as the whole Liturgy of the Word, receiving Communion every time we go to Mass, and the proclamation of the whole Eucharistic Prayer. At the same time, as I indicated in response to the previous question, historical scholarship deepened our knowledge about what was contained in those eucharistic prayers that were not the same type as the Roman Canon. It was this rigorous historical research that revealed the very important place that the Epiclesis played in the text and the proclamation of this prayer. Recall that the Epiclesis is a prayer of invocation for the transformation of bread and wine into the body and blood of Christ, and also a prayer for ever-more complete and full unity of the church. Now that the Epiclesis is an important part of nine out of ten of the eucharistic prayers in the present Missal, it is clear that we need to take this prayer seriously as an essential part of the whole Mass. Now if we Western (Roman) Catholics look at this text through an Eastern lens, we would see how logical it was for some Eastern theologians to state that it was at the Epiclesis that the bread and wine became the body and blood of Christ. After all, to state as we do in the third Eucharistic prayer—

> Therefore, O Lord, we humbly implore you:
> by the same Spirit graciously make holy
> these gifts we have brought to you for consecration,
> that they may become the Body and Blood
> of your Son our Lord Jesus Christ…

—is a pretty strong assertion that transformation is to occur now.

On the other hand, if you were a Catholic theologian through the Middle Ages and experienced the Canon without an explicit Epiclesis invoking the Holy Spirit, then it would be logical that you might argue (as most did!) that when the priest says the words of Jesus—"This is my body, this is my blood"—the bread and wine become Christ's body and blood. Now that the Epiclesis has been restored as an element of the Eucharistic Prayer, we can assert that perhaps the best way to understand *when* the consecration happens is during the Eucharistic Prayer as a whole, especially from the Epiclesis asking that the gifts be transformed, through the institution narrative, the anamnesis, and the "second" Epiclesis for church unity. This enables us not to have to make an either/or decision about the Epiclesis or the institution narrative. What it also does is to underscore the emphasis in the *General Instruction of the Roman Missal*, which continually adds the description "institution narrative" to the term *consecration*. This phrasing is the church's way of saying "appreciate what this whole text is," rather than just look at what happens as a result of its being prayed.

Lastly, as one liturgical directive of the importance of the Epiclesis *and* the institution narrative *and* the anamnesis, let's take a look at the directions for a concelebrated Mass (when one or more priests assist at Mass with the presiding priest or bishop). As you probably have noticed at these Masses, when the presiding priest or bishop begins the Epiclesis for the transformation of the bread and wine, all the other priests extend their hands (with palms down as a gesture invoking the Spirit) and say the whole central part of the Eucharistic Prayer through the end of the anamnesis with the presiding priest. This is a rubrical directive to support what I have urged here, namely, that we don't regard "this is my body...blood" as a formula to convert bread and wine into Christ's body and blood, but that we see this part of the Eucharistic Prayer in relation to the prayer as a whole as the center of the whole celebration.

Let me now add one observation from the church's prayer here about the role of the priest. Whatever view one might have taken historically about when the transformation takes place, one thing is sure: that in the Epiclesis, the phrase "by the same Holy Spirit graciously make holy these gifts we have brought to you for consecration," or any variation of it, is a theologically significant assertion that whatever we do in the liturgy is always done through the power of the Spirit—not on our own. Similarly, when the priest uses the words of Jesus from the Last Supper, "this is my body...blood," he is reminded that these words are not his, they are Christ's. This is to say that this part of the Eucharistic Prayer is different from what occurs prior to it because up to this point the phrasing in the priest's text has been in the name of the church and an address to God, such as, "To you, therefore, most merciful Father, we make humble prayer and petition..." (Roman Canon). But here, at the institution narrative, by using the words of Christ, the text reminds us that the transformation is not up to the priest himself. Rather, it is up to the very person of Christ (*in persona Christi*), whose words and actions he recalls at this part of the Mass. Again, the power to consecrate comes from Christ's words. The priest's power, in either case, is vicarious in the best sense of that term. The priest speaks and acts in the name and person of Christ—not on his own. This is a humbling reminder of who the priest is and of the overwhelming power of the Trinity at work in the action of the Mass.

The last thing I'd like to say about your question about the Consecration is that in the reformed Mass much greater emphasis is now placed on the people's reception of Communion. This shifts the emphasis away from the post-Reformation triad: Offertory, Consecration, and Communion (of the priest). That made for a valid Mass. In a technical sense it still does. But the Communion of the priest leads to the Communion of all the assembly gathered for Mass. In other words, the consecration of the elements occurs so that we can share in the transformed eucharistic gifts—Christ's body and blood. Perhaps another reason why you don't hear much about the Consecration as a distinct part of the Mass is that when we Catholics emphasized it, few of us actually received Communion. Now that most of us receive Communion every time we celebrate the Mass, it would make sense that we emphasize the act of sharing in Communion as an (equally?) important element of the Mass. After all, the purpose of the Mass is our participation (taking part) in Christ's act of salvation for us, and the consecration of the elements makes this possible through eucharistic Communion. The words of Jesus at the Last Supper are "take and eat...drink."

63. You seem to be placing a lot of emphasis on the action of the Holy Spirit in the Eucharistic Prayer and in the Mass in general. Can you really justify this since the Holy Spirit was only mentioned at the very end of the Roman Canon and therefore was not central to the Mass before Vatican II?

Your question is very significant and this topic has been very much at the forefront of recent liturgical writings. In fact, one of the reasons why I answered the previous two questions at some length is that the emphasis placed on the Holy Spirit in the texts of the prayers of the present Mass (and therefore the understanding of the Mass) is nothing short of revolutionary.

But first of all I'd like to clear up something that may be behind your question, that is, whether this emphasis on the Spirit is an indirect way of saying that the older Missal was wrong. Or, as some people put it today, if the Roman Canon was *the* Eucharistic Prayer for fifteen centuries, who are we to change it? (I am reminded here of my answer to question 18 about the notion of a "new" Mass.) The best simple answer I can give comes from a document at the very beginning of the present Missal, an apostolic constitution (meaning the highest level of a papal decree) written by Pope Paul VI authorizing the publication and use of the new Missal. This is more than a legal document insisting that the Missal be used. It is a very helpful summary of the chief features of the revised Mass. In this relatively brief text, the pope asserts that

> it should in no way be thought that this revision of the Roman Missal has been introduced without preparation, since without any doubt the way was prepared by progress in liturgical disciplines these last four centuries. After the Council of Trent, the reading and examination of "ancient manuscripts, both those in the Vatican library and others discovered elsewhere" helped not a little in the revision of the Roman Missal, as is confirmed by the Apostolic Constitution *Quo primum* issued by Our Predecessor Saint Pius V. Subsequently on the one hand very ancient liturgical sources have of course been discovered and published, and on the other hand the liturgical formularies of the Eastern Church have been studied more deeply. As a result, it has been the desire of many that...these doctrinal and spiritual riches not lie in the darkness of archives, but rather be brought out into the light to enlighten and nourish the minds and spirits of Christians. (*Missale Romanum*)

It is this contribution of recent liturgical scholarship, especially the influence of Eastern texts, that has enabled the church to put together the riches of this new Missal. In a sense then, the publication of both the Tridentine and the present Missal demonstrates that at both times the Missal then in use was corrected by the new Missal. From this authoritative statement I would argue that the addition of emphasis on the power and role of the Holy Spirit in the Mass is a legitimate advancement in the Catholic Church's prayer that is based on traditional sources and is a most legitimate advance to enhance our liturgical prayer.

Now with regard to your asking whether what we prayed in the Tridentine Missal is to be considered "wrong," I guess I'd rather use the term *inadequate*. This allows for the pride of place given to the Tridentine Missal over the centuries, and to the Canon over a thousand years older than the Tridentine Missal. Just as the Tridentine Missal improved what came before it, so the Missal of Paul VI, officially endorsed by the highest church authority and based on the liturgical scholarship of our day, helps the present church to benefit from recent liturgical study and to achieve a "less inadequate" set of prayers for the Mass. (I say *less inadequate* because we will never ever achieve a "perfect" Mass in this life!) In addition, the emphasis we now place on the Epiclesis in the Eucharistic Prayer and on the Holy Spirit in general cannot but help in ecumenical relations among all the churches—East and West. The new Missal is liturgically and theologically normative. It is called the ordinary form. From it we can develop a more and more adequate theology of the Mass from the richness of its prayers, especially those that point to the active role of the Holy Spirit in the Mass.

Much of what I have consistently argued in this book is based on what the liturgy says, and by this means to unpack what the liturgy means. The new eucharistic prayers are normative and offer a great deal to reflect on in order to understand what we do when we celebrate the Mass. The new Missal simply offers much that is new and that can be used to develop our understanding of what the Mass really means.

64. Sometimes our priest says something different at the Eucharistic Prayer and some other parts of the Mass. Is this allowed?

Let me begin by making some comments on where the Eucharistic Prayer came from in Jewish practice, as this may help us understand the notion of variety within a prayer that is sometimes legitimate and sometimes not. The religious customs of Judaism placed great value on sharing meals together with family and friends in faith. During those meals there would always be some public declaration as to why they gathered, and normally such statements included thanking God for liberation and sanctification, for example, liberation from the bondage of slavery in Egypt and the hope and promise of coming into the presence of the all holy God. The structure of such a blessing prayer included three things. The first part was a solemn declaration to "bless" God (the Hebrew root for this is *berakah*, translated as "Blessed are you, Lord God"). The second part was a declaration of thanks elaborating on why we acknowledged God in this way. The third part was a supplication, asking that the God who was blessed and thanked would continue to shower grace and favor on the chosen people. The name for this particular prayer form is (in Hebrew) the *birkat-ha-mazon*. Now the structure of this prayer form is fixed, but its content was not so fixed. It was the responsibility of the one presiding to elaborate or embellish on this structure, most especially the second part. It is this precedent or custom of elaborating within a fixed prayer form that gave rise in early Christianity for this to be the custom at Christian Eucharists or meal fellowship. Therefore, in his *Apostolic Tradition*, what Hippolytus gave to the newly ordained bishop as a Eucharistic Prayer was a fairly detailed outline—but it was an outline that he could elaborate on in light of a given feast or occasion. This precedent for variety within a structured text gave rise to the custom in the Roman Rite of having many prefaces for the Roman Canon. This is also the precedent for the fact that the Canon itself contained varied and variable parts within it. (I suspect that this precedent in the Roman Canon gave rise to the fact that the recently approved Eucharistic Prayer for Various Needs and Occasions is a prayer with four prefaces and four intercessory sections to the single prayer.)

Now, back to your question about the priest saying "something different" in the Eucharistic Prayer. Clearly he has over ninety options to choose from for the Preface. I suspect that sometimes this can seem to be "different" from what is customary. But this is perfectly legitimate.

At the risk of becoming too fussy (nobody ever likes a fussy liturgist—and probably with good reason!), let me offer a general comment and two examples of "something different" I have heard at Masses. But first let me make the general observation that, when it comes to all the texts of the liturgy, we must be very respectful of what they say because they are intended to structure a ritual of prayer that is spoken and also personal, a prayer that relies on the texts but also goes beyond the texts to foster deep, interior communion with God. When those parts of the language of the liturgy that are meant to foster this kind of deeper prayer are changed, this can disrupt what ought to be going on "under" the text. So, all things being equal, I'd be slow to change ritual texts very much at all. Now let me turn to two examples.

The first is when the priest changes a text and says something like "The Lord *is* with you" instead of "The Lord be with you," or "Let us *continue our prayer*" rather than "Let us pray." Now both of these interpolations have some merit. After all, by the time of the gospel or the Eucharistic Prayer, we have already acknowledged the Lord's presence and action among us. Hence, to assert that "the Lord *is* with" us sounds legitimate. The problem, however, is that such phrases—"The Lord be with you" and "Let us pray"—constitute what I like to call ritual language. These are key phrases in the Mass when the priest uses agreed-upon terminology in order to invite the assembly's particular attention. To change the words can invite ritual dislocation or at least some confusion among the people.

The second example concerns the change some priests make during the Eucharistic Prayer over the bread and cup. The text states that Jesus gave them to his *disciples*. However, some priests change this to his *friends*. Technically I would say that this is not a desirable change because there is a wealth of meaning behind the term *disciple*. I am thinking here of the powerful testimony of faith from the Lutheran pastor Dietrich Bonhoeffer during the Second World War entitled *The Cost of Discipleship*. I am also thinking that the Gospel of St. Matthew is really a manual for what it means to be a disciple; after all, the Greek term for *Matthew* literally means "disciple." And at the very end of that gospel, Jesus commands the eleven disciples to go forth and "make disciples" (Matt 28:16–19). These examples would lead me not to change this term because I would interpret the Eucharist here as the food to make us disciples less imperfect and more faithful followers of Jesus.

At the same time, however, I'd like to point out that, in the eucharistic prayers for Masses with children, instead of the word *disciples* these prayers use the term *friends*. Now it is obvious that *friends* has been used here to suit the comprehension of children. But it is also clear that the term is not the same as *disciple* and that *disciple* carries a great deal more theological weight. However, given the fact that there are three eucharistic prayers for children's comprehension, then we might well look at the use of *friends* as an example of intimacy, friendship, and meal fellowship. The background here is the fact that in Judaism when one shared a meal at table, one affirmed the most intimate of relationships with others (hence the depth of Judas's betrayal, which was executed by one who shared a meal at table with Jesus). The use of *friends* might well be explained in these Masses with children to underscore one of the aspects of every Mass—an intimate union with God through the action of the Mass. Clearly the customary usage in the Roman Rite at the institution narrative is usually *disciples*, but sometimes it can be *friends*, which variation is in the text of the Roman Rite itself. If the priest changes *disciples* to *friends* at Mass, I would think that he wants to stress the intimacy of what is occurring. In this case, I'd say let it go and appreciate that many terms in the liturgy have a number of very legitimate meanings.

65. The priest used to say that Christ's blood was shed for "all," but now he says it was shed for "many." Why?

The question you raise has been the subject of much debate from the beginning of experiencing the Mass in the vernacular. You are quite correct in observing that in both the Tridentine Mass and the present Latin Order of Mass, the text of the eucharistic prayers contains the phrase *pro multis effundetur*—"for many." This is from the Last Supper account in the Gospel of Matthew (26:28), which itself refers back to the Servant Song in Isaiah 53:12–13, which uses "for the many" (and which is read as the first reading on Good Friday, the Liturgy of the Lord's Passion). The literal translation is "for many," and you will find this in the standard translations of the New Testament. However, the more accurate way to translate any foreign language is to study the thought-world from which phrases and words come from, especially to see whether there are "terms behind the terms" that need to be explained and explored for the sake of accurate translation.

Let me offer an example that ties what I have been saying about this part of the Mass to American holidays. Every year on the last Monday of May, we Americans celebrate Memorial Day when we honor those who gave their lives in war for our freedom. It is a day of recalling to mind and heart those beloved dead who gave the supreme sacrifice for our country. Most of us appreciate this as the origin and meaning of this special civil holiday. However, if you were to take that same term *memorial* and put it back into the vocabulary of biblical times, you would soon discover that it meant a communal liturgical action whereby the people invoked God's gracious favor on their behalf in light of the covenant. We invoke God's activity among us now, the very same gracious action that the God of the covenant gave to all our ancestors in the faith. Also, the sense of chronological time is collapsed in the Hebraic notion of *memorial* because it includes past, present, and future all at the same time! We invoke God's blessings in the present on the basis of past marvelous deeds, and as we look to their fulfillment in the kingdom of heaven. Similarly, when we use the biblical phrase asking God to "forget" our sins, we beg God's mercy to take them away as though they had no existence. Obviously we are not asking God to engage in a mental activity—we are asking God to do something for us here and now. Now that's a lot of baggage for the simple word *memorial*. But we need to understand this rich term with its many meanings so that we can more accurately translate it liturgically and appreciate its theological depth.

The same thing is true for the term *pro multis*. The Latin here relies on the Greek and the Greek phrase is *peri pollon*, meaning (literally) "for the many," as opposed to "for a few." But what is behind each of these languages is the Semitic understanding where the word *many* may seem to be exclusive of some persons whereas in actuality it means every person except Jesus himself. Hence, the translation should be for "all" and not "many," where "many" can mean a few.

At the same time, in the previous edition of the *Sacramentary for Mass*, the English translation was initially "for all men." Then in 1980, the Congregation for Divine Worship in Rome agreed to allow the American versions of the Eucharistic prayers to read "for all." And now, with our present translation returning to the original Latin and Greek, we will have our work cut out for us for a few years to catechize people on the depth of meaning in "for many."

66. What are the correct postures during the Eucharistic Prayer?

Talk about a controversial question today! Allow me to begin with some ideas about what gestures mean at the Mass and some historical observations on how they evolved over the centuries. Then I'll tackle the state of the question in America today.

One of the principles I use to teach my students about liturgy is that all liturgical prayer is *enacted ritual*. By this I mean that it is

fundamentally an action, an event, an experience of salvation. It is
not an idea: it is not thinking about salvation. It is God's saving
presence and sanctifying action made real for us here and now. It is
also a ritual in the sense that what we do in liturgy is structured,
and in being structured it is familiar. In other words, we know how
to participate by words, gestures, and actions because they don't
change. Now one of the reasons why I find the phrase *enacted ritual* useful is that this phrase betrays the fact that all who participate
in the liturgy do so as humans—with minds, hearts, and *bodies*. Our
bodily actions, gestures, and processions at Mass all reflect the fact
that we are enfleshed human beings and that we use our bodies at
Mass to reflect just who we are. The way we act in human life—
through speech, feelings, gestures, and movement—is the way we
act in liturgy. We use all our human faculties in the liturgy in such
a way that the liturgy respects who we are as humans and in fact
emphasizes who we are as enfleshed human beings, because the
way we honor God is through the very gift God gave us—body,
mind, and heart.

Now, when you apply this to the Mass, what is clear is that the
way we use our bodies reflects the way we look at ourselves before
God. What we do in liturgy makes a theological statement. Therefore,
it is important to understand what believers in generations before us
thought about the Mass as they engaged in particular ritual gestures
during it. When we learn, for example, that the earliest Christians
through the early Middle Ages stood for the Eucharistic Prayer, we
need to look at their teaching about the Eucharist to discover the
relationship between posture and theology. In fact, there was a harmony between standing as a sign of attention, a sign of respect, and
(more theologically) a sign that we have risen with Christ and are a
resurrected, redeemed people, and the theology of the Eucharist as an
act of the pilgrim church raising minds, hearts, and bodies in communal praise and thanksgiving. Sometimes standing was accompanied
with raised hands in the prayer position called *orans* (Latin for "praying"). Hence, in these centuries, standing and raising hands at the
Eucharistic Prayer signified the attitude that the church was on its

way to the kingdom and that the Mass was a time for the whole community to join in ritual words and gestures in order to praise and thank God together.

By the time of the Middle Ages, we see certain shifts in theology and in the postures people adopted at Mass. Beginning in the ninth century, theologians began to debate what the Eucharist was and how best to describe the change from bread and wine into the body and blood of Christ. At the same time, laypeople began to show honor to the host and chalice with gestures of reverence. So did the priest. Hence, we find more attention given to describing what the eucharistic species of consecrated bread and wine was and the positive effects it would give to us. More and more the Canon came to be recited softly, then eventually it was said in silence. At this time the ritual gestures of the priest developed to show reverence to the consecrated bread and wine—namely, he would genuflect before them and eventually would raise them up for all to see. (In fact the main reason why people wanted to see the host and chalice was that they no longer received Communion regularly at Mass and so felt that this substitute, called "ocular communion," would at least satisfy their spirituality even when they didn't receive Communion. What is important about these gestures is that they also reflect the way humans communicate: the act of holding the host and chalice for people to see and the act of seeing by the people.) This custom led to the rubrics in the Tridentine Missal that the laypeople would kneel for most of the Mass. By then the emphasis was placed on the Mass as the unbloody sacrifice of Calvary, which we were privileged to experience through kneeling during most of the Mass. Because the Eucharist was so "awesome," and people watched it as spectators from the Middle Ages on, it is no surprise that great emphasis was placed on kneeling as a sign of adoration.

Now, let me make a distinction here between gestures during the Eucharistic Prayer at Mass and gestures at other times. We have evidence that even when people stood for the Eucharistic Prayer in the early church, they would bow or prostrate themselves at other times at certain liturgies, specifically on Good Friday when they would venerate the cross of Christ. This precedent then led to the custom of bowing before the Eucharist when people would venerate it outside of the Mass. Therefore, we need to keep in mind that some gestures that are fitting for devotion outside of Mass may not be fitting for the Mass itself, principally because devotions are to the eucharistic species reserved for Communion and adoration, whereas the postures assumed at Mass should reflect the theology of the eucharistic action.

This leads finally to the present state of the reform of the liturgy. The *General Instruction of the Roman Missal* (n. 44) states:

> They should kneel (*genuflectant*), on the other hand, at the Consecration, except when prevented on occasion by ill health, or for reasons of lack of space, of the large number of people present, or for another reasonable cause. However, those who do not kneel ought to make a profound bow when the Priest genuflects after the Consecration.

Examples of lack of space could be churches that have no kneelers or a large pilgrimage gathering, for example, at an outdoor sports stadium. And there are times when an individual's ill health would make this impossible. This text is immediately followed (again n. 44) by:

> It is for the Conference of Bishops, in accordance with the norm of law, to adapt the gestures and bodily postures described in the Order of Mass to the culture and reasonable traditions of peoples. However, attention must be paid to ensuring that such adaptations correspond to the meaning and character of each part of the celebration. Where it is the practice for the people to remain kneeling after the *Sanctus* (*Holy, Holy, Holy*) until the end of the Eucharistic Prayer and before Communion when the

Priest says *Ecce Agnus Dei* (*This is the Lamb of God*), it is laudable for this practice to be retained.

Further, this is an instance where the diocesan bishop may have additional instructions about posture. The adage "when in Rome, do as the Romans do" certainly applies here.

My experience of the ritual gesture of standing was that it enabled people to be engaged in the Eucharistic Prayer that captured their minds and hearts as a prayer of praise and thanks of a pilgrim church in a way that is not always common when people kneel for this prayer. In most parishes where I now celebrate Mass, I note a distinct change in attention and focus when people kneel after the Holy, Holy, Holy. What happens often when they kneel is that they bow their heads in reverence and adoration and seem to be less engaged in the words and action of the Eucharistic Prayer and the eucharistic action itself. Despite my pastoral experience, I would side with the custom of following the Roman Missal as it is so that the already agreed-upon postures and gestures for the Mass build up the Body of Christ. As the *General Instruction of the Roman Missal* puts it (n. 42):

> A common bodily posture, to be observed by all those taking part, is a sign of the unity of the members of the Christian community gathered together for the sacred Liturgy, for it expresses the intentions and spiritual attitude of the participants and also fosters them.

67. I have read that we have "taken the sacrifice out of the Mass." Is this true? Doesn't the Eucharistic Prayer refer to the sacrifice of the Mass?

My sense is that the rhetoric about "taking the sacrifice out of the Mass" really is a way for some people to complain that the celebration of the ordinary form of the Mass is not the same as the extraordinary form. What I'd like to suggest is that the present Missal seeks to combine the notions of meal, eucharistic action, and sacrament with what was the predominant emphasis in the previous Missal, namely, that of the Mass as a sacrifice. The facts that the Offertory prayers in the Tridentine Missal were severely reduced in number and the gestures almost eliminated may cause some to view the sacrificial aspect of the Mass as diminished. In addition, the fact that the priest normally faces us during the Mass can emphasize our visual appreciation of the Mass as a sacred, ritual meal, as opposed to the priest not facing us and our watching for the elevation (as in the Tridentine Mass). But I'd like to turn the tables here and offer the observation that in fact the new Missal places *more* emphasis on the sacrificial aspect of the Mass at the words of institution than the Tridentine Missal did. Let me explain.

In the Tridentine Missal, the consecration formula for the priest was "This is my body." (For those of us old enough to remember the Latin, especially us servers, we heard *hoc est enim corpus meum*.) In the present Missal, this text has been expanded in all the eucharistic prayers added since Vatican II to read "This is my body which will be given up for you." The scripture sources for both of these texts are the accounts of the Last Supper in the gospels. The source for the text in the Tridentine Missal is Matthew 26:26, and for the present Missal the source is Luke 22:19. The principal reason offered as to why the new Missal contains the added phrase "given for you" is that it emphasizes Christ's sacrificial death and resurrection commemorated in the Eucharist for us. The declaration "This is my body" may well carry this association, but it is certainly not explicit. So the editors of the new Missal sought to emphasize the sacrificial aspect of the Mass at the precise place where it was emphasized classically— at the words over the bread. So on this one, I'd say that the new Missal in fact does a better job of linking Jesus' words at the Last Supper with our appreciation of the Mass as sacrifice.

In addition, in the present eucharistic prayers there are several explicit references to offering the eucharistic sacrifice. Among these are the classic words of the Roman Canon: "We offer to you, God of glory and majesty, this holy and perfect sacrifice, the bread of life and the cup of eternal salvation." Also in Eucharistic Prayer IV, we pray:

> Look, O Lord, look upon the Sacrifice
> which you yourself have provided for your Church,
> and grant in your loving kindness
> to all who partake in this one Bread and one Chalice
> that, gathered into one body by the Holy Spirit,
> they may truly become a living sacrifice in Christ
> to the praise of your glory.

This latter example is particularly poignant and important because it reminds us that we ourselves are to become spiritual sacrifices in the sense that we offer ourselves in service to others (from Rom 12:1–21). Again, what we find here is ample evidence that what we do at the liturgy should be reflected in the way we live our lives. What Christ did once for all was to offer himself as saving sacrifice for our salvation. What remains to be seen is how well we in fact sacrifice ourselves for the sake of others.

One last comment about the structure of the Mass, and this goes back to the rites at the Preparation of the Gifts. The first proposal for the new Mass eliminated all the prayers said over the bread and wine as well as the invitation "Pray, brethren" with the response "May the Lord accept the sacrifice…" One of the reasons given why this invitation and response was put back into the Missal and remains part of the Mass is precisely because some who evaluated the new Mass thought that the sacrificial elements had been eclipsed too much. The reinsertion of the texts "that my sacrifice and yours may be acceptable" and "may the Lord accept the sacrifice" was one way of assuaging the critics of the new Missal. In short, I'd say that there is ample textual and ritual evidence that reflects our belief that the Mass is a sacrifice. But there is also ample evidence to reflect the nature of the Mass as sacrament, meal, and table fellowship with other believers in *communion*, that is, union with God and with one another in Christ.

VII

Communion Rite

68. Given all the options, why is it that the Lord's Prayer is sung or said at every Mass? And why does the priest use the word *dare* in the introduction to it?

Let me begin by underscoring your assertion about the place of the Lord's Prayer at Mass (and at other liturgies revised since Vatican II). This prayer is often referred to as a perfect introduction to the Rite of Communion, for what we pray is what we now enact. We address God as Father using the words Christ gave us. We have just completed the Eucharistic Prayer, when we join the priest in offering Christ's paschal mystery and ourselves through, with, and in him to God the Father, in the unity (communion) of the church in the Holy Spirit. Now we pray in the words that Jesus gave us. This structure is typical of Jewish prayers: naming, addressing, and praising God ("hallowed be thy name"), making seven petitions (the number was customary at special Jewish feasts), and ending with a final doxology "for the kingdom, the power, and the glory are yours…." The two particularly notable features of this at Mass are that we ask God to "forgive us our trespasses as we forgive those who trespass against us," and that we pray "give us this day our daily bread." Therefore, when prayed as part of the Rite of Communion at Mass, the Our Father can be taken to refer to the act of Communion ("daily bread") to come. In addition, the petition "thy kingdom come" can serve as a helpful reminder that every Mass looks to the next one, and all of them look to their fulfillment and completion in the kingdom in eternity. So even as we look to partaking in broken bread and wine poured out at the Eucharist on a given day, at this point in the Mass we also pray for the fulfillment of this Mass and of all human life by seeking fulfillment and completion in the kingdom of heaven.

This prayer also has had a distinct role in the Liturgy of the Hours, Rites of Penance, and so on. Because it has been classically understood as the model Christian prayer, it has been restored as the conclusion to the Intercessions at Morning and Evening Prayer. It has also been restored to a place of emphasis and importance in the Rites of Communal Penance. We pray this prayer together as we are about to confess our sins and receive absolution. Again, the key idea here is *forgiveness*—from God as well as for and from one another. This same holds true for its place as part of the Rites of Communion.

And about the word *dare* in the Roman Rite's introduction to the Lord's Prayer: "At the Savior's command and formed by divine teaching, we dare to say...." The sense of this invitation is that we acknowledge that we really are unworthy of what we are engaged in, especially as we pray the words of Jesus and partake in this sacred meal, and that it is only through God's grace that we "dare" (*audemus*) to say these words. In fact, there is something very bold about addressing God as Our Father. *Dare to say* underscores this, while at the same time inviting us to pray these very important words.

69. In my parish we hold hands during the Our Father, but lately I have heard that this is a problem. Can you explain?

In answering the question about postures during the Eucharistic Prayer (number 66), I mentioned in passing the value of appreciating how our bodies are used in worship and that gestures, movement, postures, and processions are all part of worship, specifically the Mass. I would also say that overall we simply haven't got it right, or as right as we could or might get it. In fact, I'd go so far as to argue that, in the adoption of the reformed liturgy in the United States, we've done fairly well in implementing what takes place at the altar ("in the sanctuary," as we used to say) and that ministers are well trained for the proclamation of the Word and the distribution of the Eucharist. But what leaves a lot to be desired is the full, bodily involvement in the action of the Mass by the congregation, specifically in the Introductory Rites, at the Presentation of the Gifts, and during the Rites of Communion. I urge that we evaluate the quality of our liturgical participation, not only by the words and the gestures of the ministers, but also by how the whole assembly involves itself through postures, symbolic actions, and movement, as well as words.

Now to your precise question. Let me go back again to the response to question 66 where I spoke about the ancient Christian custom of praying in the standing posture with arms raised and palms open to the heavens. This is called the *orans* position, from the Latin for the "praying" posture. One of the traditional places during Mass when the whole assembly assumed the *orans* position was during the praying of the Lord's Prayer. This gesture then led to the community's exchanging the Sign of Peace—another extremely important ritual gesture. Given the tradition behind the *orans* position as an appropriate posture for the Lord's Prayer and the value that the liturgy has traditionally placed on gestures, it is common for many members of the congregation to extend their hands in the *orans* position, which I deem a very appropriate use of the body in worship. However, after the post–Vatican II reform of the Mass, what happened was that some American parishes instead adopted the gesture of holding hands during the Lord's Prayer. This obviously signified solidarity and reflected how the Rites of Communion concerned our relationship with one another as well as our relationship with God through Christ in the act of taking Communion.

But let's examine the gestures of the Rites of Communion as a whole, and let's take a look at the text of the Lord's Prayer itself. Clearly, what we have here is series of gestures that should reflect our speaking to God and our communicating with one another. While the text of the Lord's Prayer refers both to God and to one another ("as we forgive those who trespass against us"), we must admit that it primarily concerns what we ask of God through Christ in seven petitions, after we have named God as Father and invoked praise by saying "hallowed be thy name." For this reason alone, some commentators have observed that we should "revisit" the practice of holding hands in favor of emphasizing the *orans* position here. (In fact, the same argument could be made for reintroducing the *orans* position for the whole assembly during the Eucharistic Prayer while they are standing.) If the assembly were to assume the *orans* position at the Lord's Prayer and then exchange the Sign of Peace, the result would be a balance of bodily involvement—referring both to God and to one another.

The last thing I want to do is to diminish the assembly's liturgical participation through gestures and postures. But I would like to call for a "mid-course correction" that might make our bodily involvement the better thought-out and reflect a theology through gesture that refers both to God and to one another.

70. Why don't we say "for the kingdom, the power, and the glory are yours..." right after the Our Father? Wouldn't it be more correct, at least ecumenically?

Thank you for making the connection (which not everyone makes) between the phrase "for the kingdom, the power, and the glory are yours..." in the present Catholic Missal and the more common translation used by other Christian churches: "for thine is the kingdom, and the power, and the glory forever...." Both of these texts serve as doxologies to conclude the Lord's Prayer. Some scripture commentators have suggested that this would have been the logical conclusion of a prayer such as the Our Father, just as our Eucharistic Prayer ends with the Doxology "through him...all glory and honor is yours almighty Father, forever and ever. Amen." The structure here would follow Jewish liturgical prayers where petitions are set within a prayer that begins and ends with explicit praise of God. Regarding the doxologies you indicate, there are ecumenical implications here that might be better served if we all said the same thing at the same time.

Historically, the difference was caused by the translation of the New Testament from its original Greek into other languages, specifically German and Latin. At the time of the Reformation, Martin Luther undertook the Herculean task of translating the scriptures into German, and this is his rendering of the Doxology at the conclusion of the Lord's Prayer. However, when St. Jerome translated the New Testament from Greek into Latin (what we call the Vulgate), he did not include this Doxology to end the Lord's Prayer. Since from the time of St. Jerome on, Catholics translated the scriptures from the Vulgate, so it is not surprising that this Doxology was not included in such translations or in the Latin Mass texts. (At the risk of oversimplification, we might say that what was thought to be a Protestant-Catholic split was really a matter of whose scripture translation you used. If you used Jerome's, there was no Doxology. If you used Luther's, there was a Doxology. It took a thousand years for this to become an ecumenical issue!)

To answer the question: first, while the American bishops have adopted a number of suggestions put forth for common texts for the Christian churches, they have not adopted the "ecumenical" translation of the Lord's Prayer. Why? Certainly it is not to diminish the value of prayers that the Christian churches have in common. It is really a pastoral judgment. The fact that people know this prayer by heart and have been taught the phrasing in the Missal led the bishops to judge it best to keep it as it was.

Regarding the seeming dislocation of the Doxology in the Catholic Mass as opposed to saying it immediately at the end of the Lord's Prayer, let me offer a bit of liturgical history and precedent from the evolution of the Roman Rite. After the final words of the Lord's Prayer in the Roman Rite, "but deliver us from evil," it was customary for the priest or bishop to elaborate on this phrase by a text (originally of his own composition) that came to be called the *embolism* to the Our Father. This embolism drew out one or another theme from the previous phrase in light of the feast or season, or in light of the fact that we are about to exchange the Sign of Peace. Therefore, what gradually emerged in the Roman Rite was the establishment of the fixed embolism that we hear in the revised Mass. Note that its first words echo the words of the Our

Father: "deliver us from evil" leads to "deliver us, Lord, we pray, from every evil...." The petition to "graciously grant peace in our day" is a subtle introduction to the Sign of Peace to follow. The time frame—"as we await the blessed hope and the coming of our Savior, Jesus Christ"—is particularly significant as once again the eschatological ("not yet") character of all worship (and the whole Christian life) is underscored. We await Christ's return in glory to bring time to an end. How fitting, therefore, that the Doxology itself should end with coupling "now and forever."

Despite these differences of exactly where the Doxology occurs, I think it must be admitted that its insertion into the Missal so everyone can hear the embolism is significant and that the addition of the Doxology for all to pray is also a significant, if small, step toward ecumenical unity. In addition, the fact that the embolism has found a place in the Roman Rite since the early centuries and is part of our Catholic tradition makes me want to at least name this as a "Catholic" value and practice whose theology is significant: peace, eschatology, and doxology all in one!

71. Is the priest supposed to invite us to exchange the Sign of Peace at every Mass? Should he come down to the congregation to exchange it with us?

Among the reforms of the Mass after Vatican II, the restoration of the Sign of Peace was one that drew a lot of attention and some heated debate! One obvious reason was that it asked congregations to engage other persons around them at the very time when they customarily would be praying silently before receiving Communion (as they watched the priest receive Communion). The Sign of Peace, despite its name, caused no little upheaval!

Historically we know that the whole assembly joined in exchanging the Sign of Peace as a ritual gesture signifying unity, reconciliation, and a deepening share in Christ's peace. However, just as many of the ritual gestures that "belonged" to the people came to be engaged in by the priest and other ministers only. According to the rubrics for the extraordinary form of the Mass, after the breaking of the bread and the acclamation "Lamb of God...," the priest says the prayer that we now have: "Lord Jesus Christ, you said to your apostles I leave you peace, my peace I give to you...." Then if the Sign of Peace is to be offered, he kisses the altar (the symbol of Christ himself) and gives the peace to the deacon who gives it in turn to the subdeacon, who in turn exchanges it with other ministers and eventually the people in a chain-like procedure.

The new Missal rearranged part of the Communion Rite so that after the Doxology "for the kingdom, the power, and the glory are yours," the priest says the "Lord Jesus Christ" prayer, greets the entire assembly with the text "The peace of the Lord be with you always," and follows it with the exchange of the Sign of Peace. Now this is where the answer to your precise question lies. In the Missal it states, "Then, if appropriate, the Deacon, or the Priest, adds...'Let us offer each other the Sign of Peace.'" So to the first part of your question the Missal says that the priest or deacon decides when it is appropriate for the assembly to exchange the Sign of Peace. However, given our liturgical history, it would seem most appropriate to exchange it on a regular basis. This ritual gesture can signify our relatedness in Christ and to each other that has been solidified in the celebration of Mass itself.

Other interesting changes in this rite from the Tridentine Mass are that the priest no longer kisses the altar and that the people exchange the Sign of Peace among themselves. The rationale here is that the assembly of believers is itself a sign of the presence of Christ, and hence the Body of Christ can and should share the peace of Christ with one another without having to wait for the peace to "come from the sanctuary." I think this is important so that the assembly experience in this way their baptismal identity and relatedness to one another in and through Christ present in the gathered assembly. Now with regard to the nature of the gesture to be used, the Missal states that this is done "according to local custom." In most parishes I'd say that the handshake is the most common gesture. For some, the embrace might be a better gesture. For families, even a kiss itself might be most appropriate. If the handclasp is used, one suggestion from the American Bishops' Committee on the Liturgy statement on "The Sign of Peace" (1977) is that we might consider using two hands to shake the hands of our neighbor. This would signify a deeper commitment to the other than the handclasp that is common in ordinary business and social life. After all, what we wish is that the peace *of Christ* might take deeper root and be a source of reconciliation and a deeper experience of God's favor and grace.

As to whether the priest should come down to the congregation, the revised edition of the *General Instruction of the Roman Missal* offers the following directives. The general statement is that it is appropriate "that each person offer the Sign of Peace only to those who are nearest and in a sober manner" (n. 82). Then it specifies the following for the priest: "The Priest may give the Sign of Peace to the ministers but always remains within the sanctuary, so that the celebration is not disrupted. He should do the same if for a reasonable cause he wishes to offer the Sign of Peace to a small number of the faithful" (n. 154). In the document "The Sign of Peace," the value of having the people exchange this gesture with each other is upheld, with the caution that if the clergy try to "reach out and touch" everyone, or even the majority of the assembly, then this could come across as heavily weighted in favor of a clerical imposition. My own sense is that the most important phrase in this directive is "so that the celebration is not disrupted." This means that reverence and decorum—which should mark the entire liturgy—is to be evident as we do engage one another with this important ritual gesture.

72. When should the Sign of Peace be exchanged—at its present place, at the Penitential Rite, or at the Presentation of the Gifts?

In the earliest evidence we have of the Roman liturgy (Justin the Martyr and Hippolytus, for example), the Sign of Peace was exchanged at the time of the Presentation of the Gifts. Then by the fourth century it was changed to its present location before the reception of Communion. It was never at the Introductory Rites. Let me try to explain why it was where it has been and why it would not be in the Introductory Rites of the Mass.

The principal reason why the Sign of Peace was first exchanged after the Liturgy of the Word and before the gifts were presented was to conform with Jesus' teaching in the Gospel of Matthew (5:23–24): "Therefore, if you bring your gift to the altar, and there recall that your brother has anything against you, leave your gift there at the altar, go first and be reconciled with your brother, and then come and offer your gift." Not surprisingly, purity of intention should match the giving of the gift, and a deep integration of what is celebrated and what is lived makes the offering of worship the more desirable. The fact that this was the location of the Sign of Peace in the West, and remains the location for it in many Eastern Rites to this day, is the reason why the theology of the proclaimed Word is often cited as the basis for our reconciliation. What God offers us through the proclaimed Word—the good news of salvation in Christ—is to be offered to each other in worship and in life. What God "creates" through the proclaimed and preached Word is to become reality in human life.

In the West by the fourth century, however, the exchanging of the Sign of Peace shifted to its present location. Among others, St. Augustine offers a theological explanation as to why it is located after the Lord's Prayer and before Communion. In one of his sermons (n. 227), he indicates that the gesture of the Sign of Peace requires that worshipers demonstrate through this sign what they have just prayed: "forgive us...as we forgive." He also indicates that it is appropriate that, after we have exchanged the Sign of Peace, we then approach sacramental Communion and receive the Body of Christ, which term for Augustine refers both to the eucharistic species in Communion and to the church as Christ's body (from the poignant metaphor from St. Paul in 1 Corinthians). Hence, the present location of the sign can be considered traditional from the fourth century on in the Roman Rite, and the gesture itself should be understood in relation to the praying of the Our Father and receiving Communion.

On the basis of these strong liturgical precedents and the theological reasoning behind them, I'd be hard pressed to think that the Sign of Peace should be exchanged as part of the Introductory Rites. What we now call the Act of Penitence originated as the priest's private prayers of devotion said in the sacristy before the Mass began. Hence, the weight we should give to it is minor compared with the proclamation of the Word and the eucharistic action itself. Now what does occur on some occasions is that, before Mass begins, a commentator will address the assembly and invite them to greet each other. This is done in the spirit of part of what the Introductory Rites are to accomplish as stated in the *General Instruction of the Roman Missal*, n. 46: "Their purpose is to ensure that the faithful who come together as one, establish communion and dispose themselves properly to listen to the word of God and to celebrate the Eucharist worthily." (For more on this see chapter 4, "Introductory Rites.") This kind of greeting could enhance the sense of belonging to a community when in fact the congregation that comes together is disparate and they have come together for a particular occasion, for example, at the celebration of sacraments such as marriage, ordination, baptism, and confirmation.

73. Why does the priest mingle a small piece of the consecrated host into the cup? What is its significance?

It may come as a surprise at first but the principal reason why part of the consecrated bread is dropped into the chalice has to do with church unity! Let me give some theological background and historical precedents for it.

Every act of liturgy is done for the sake of those present and for the whole church throughout the world. That's why, for example, the petitions in the Universal Prayer always stretch us to intercede for the concerns of the whole church and the wider world.

Another way that this universal dimension of the Mass is under-scored is by the inclusion of prayers for the unity and peace of the church (often in the Prayers over the Gifts and the Prayer after Communion). Now another way that the liturgy signifies the uni-versality of what we celebrate is through what was originally called the Rite of the *Fermentum* (meaning a particle of consecrated bread). Pope Innocent I in the fifth century wrote that, because of the large numbers of Christians in Rome, they all could not gather together for the pope's Eucharist on a given Sunday. Hence, the pope would send acolytes from the papal Sunday Mass with parts of the eucharistic bread that he had consecrated in order that the pastors of Rome's parish churches would place this eucharistic bread in the chalice at the Mass they were celebrating. This was done as an important sign of unity and communion with the pope's Mass. So this seemingly insignificant gesture carried associ-ations of church unity, relationship with the pope, the theology of Sunday as *the* day to gather for Mass, and so on.

The *fermentum* was not sent to the rural parishes (because of distance), however, and the many other parishes of the Christian world began to adopt another custom that replicated this rite, at least in some way. This was called the *sancta* and it more closely resembles what you see at Mass now, but not exactly! What began to happen was that priests on their own would take a particle of the consecrated bread and place it on the altar at the time of the breaking of the bread. He would leave it there until the next Mass that was celebrated at that altar. At that next Mass the priest would drop this particle of bread into the chalice and alternatively leave a fragment for the next Mass, and so on. The theology of church unity is reflected in this rite but now it emphasized how one Mass leads to the next Mass, until the kingdom comes. The principal theological reason is that the Mass is never solely for those who gather for it as though it were a "closed club." The Mass is always for believers in the whole church, and at every Mass those who gather intercede for the church throughout the world and for the needs of the whole world.

74. Some priests change the words that invite us to receive Communion. Can you explain?

According to the Missal, at the invitation to Communion the priest says:

> Behold the Lamb of God,
> behold him who takes away the sins of the world.
> Blessed are those called to the supper of the Lamb.

Sometimes you might hear the words "happy are we who are called to this supper/table" or other variations. What I'd like to suggest as I try to explain the difference is that many of the texts we use in the liturgy have more than one meaning, even though one meaning might be more apparent than another. The principle here is called *multivalence*. If you have any familiarity with chemistry (and here my high school chemistry teacher would either cringe about what I'm going to say or be proud that I at least did remember this!) is that part of it was based on the periodic chart of *valences,* which word signifies "meaning" or "meanings." When you add the prefix *multi-* (from the Latin *multis,* meaning "many"), then this term is a shorthand way of saying that sometimes the words we use at Mass have many meanings. The priest's statement just before Communion is one such text with many meanings.

The text at this point in the Missal ("Blessed are those called to the supper of the Lamb") is taken from the Book of Revelation 19:9, prefiguring the end of time when the "elect" are called to eternal union with God. The imagery here is of being called to the wedding feast in the kingdom of heaven. Therefore, what the priest says here is both an invitation to Communion now and a reminder of being called to the banquet of the Lamb in the kingdom of heaven. When the Missal uses the pronoun *those,* it quotes Revelation and refers to all those who one day will experience eternal life. Again, the technical term for this kind of statement is that it is *eschatological.* Essentially this kind of prayer is a reminder that our ultimate goal is eternal life in heaven. The precise metaphor for it in the Book of Revelation is that we hope to join all those who are called to "the supper of the Lamb." It signifies that what we do at Mass is meant to lead to its final consummation at the eternal banquet with God in heaven.

Now in the present Roman Rite, we have very few such references to this eschatological aspect of the Eucharist. Probably the major reason is that our Roman Catholic theology of eucharistic presence, of sacrifice and offering, and of the intercessory power of the Mass grew in importance over the centuries in light of the debates at the Reformation. Therefore, it is not surprising that our present Missal should continue to emphasize the power of what we do "here and now." But there is always a dimension of the Mass signifying that "we are not there yet" and that there is a kind of promise of what we shall experience in its fullness in the kingdom of heaven.

When the priest changes words such as *they* to *we*, and *his supper* to *this supper*, what he is doing is emphasizing that this is an invitation to take Communion at this Mass. But that is really only part of what this text means: it also means that what we share here and now will lead us to a sharing in the eternal, heavenly banquet in eternity. Strictly speaking, therefore, there is great merit to keeping the text as it is, so that its many meanings about coming to this Communion and to the eternal banquet can be conveyed by the single phrase from the Book of Revelation.

But for the sake of completion and nuance, I need to point out that in some of the Eastern Rites, the text for the invitation to Communion contains the phrase *holy things for the holy*. This suggests that what we take in Communion is to make us, the baptized people of God, God's "holy ones," the more holy through this act of eucharistic Communion. I'd also say that this phrase from the Eastern Rites is quite legitimate because at this part of the Mass we are invited to Communion. But the reason why I'd like to keep the clear eschatological phrasing in our present Roman Missal is that, unlike the Eastern Rites, we refer to this "not yet" aspect of the Eucharist in very few places. The Eastern Rites, however, have strong emphases in this direction in the texts and rites of their liturgy of the Mass. On balance, I think we in the West can learn an important lesson here from the East.

75. Why do some people kneel on one knee before receiving Communion?

There are a number of issues at stake here when you describe the gesture of kneeling "on one knee" and the proper manner of receiving Communion. Let me begin by making a distinction between kneeling and genuflecting. Normally the posture of kneeling means to remain for some time on one's knees (usually both). This was the most common gesture assumed by the congregation during the Tridentine Mass. The gesture of a genuflection, however, signifies touching the floor with one knee and assuming the standing position immediately thereafter. So I suspect that what you are referring to is the genuflection that some people engage in as they approach to receive Communion. I say *some* people because, as you suggest in your question, this has not been stipulated as a gesture that all must perform.

The *General Instruction of the Roman Missal* (n. 160) states "the faithful communicate either kneeling or standing, as has been determined by the norms of the Conference of Bishops. However, when they communicate standing, it is recommended that before receiving the Sacrament they make an appropriate sign of reverence, to be determined in the same norms."

The American bishops have decided that the normal posture for receiving Communion is standing and that reception is preceded by a bow of the head. The same procedure is observed both for the consecrated bread and the precious blood. They also state that if a person received while kneeling, Communion should not be refused and the communicant should be catechized about the standing posture.

To your direct question, then, I would say that the present norms do not allow for a genuflection before Communion. I think it important to hold to the standing posture for at least three reasons. Liturgical gestures are meant to be communal expressions and are determined in the liturgical books. Conforming to them should not be seen as restrictive. Rather, it should be instructive so that the liturgy can be carried out with reverence and decorum with everyone knowing what is expected of them. The second reason is that if persons genuflect when walking to Communion this can cause others to walk into them, not realizing that they would adopt this posture. The third reason is that some might judge genuflecting before receiving, or receiving while kneeling, to be more reverent and they should have the right to assume that posture. This is not our judgment to make. The American bishops have made the decision that bowing and standing are the postures.

76. Is it more reverent to receive Communion on the tongue?

Let me begin by recalling what I said in response to question 66 (about the postures for the Eucharistic Prayer)—specifically, that a principle of liturgy is that in it we use our bodies to express what we say and do at Mass. Then, in response to the previous question, I cited the directives about the reverence to be given through our bodies to this part of the Mass. Now, your question asks the more precise question: Which is the better way to receive Communion— on the tongue or "in the hand"?

In summarizing some liturgical history in this response, I'd like to combine the evidence of what people *did* to show their reverence to the Eucharist with what they understood the Eucharist to be. This may help explain where we have come from and the rationale for why we have two options for the way we can receive Communion today. One of the main sources for explanations about the rites of the Mass and their theological meanings from the fourth and fifth centuries are documents called *mystagogic catecheses*. Now that first word *mystagogic* has recently returned to our church vocabulary by way of the Rite of Christian Initiation of Adults. After adults have received sacramental initiation, they now experience a period of "unpacking" what has happened to them, and this is called the period of *mystagogy*. This term is taken from the Greek and means "to be instructed in the mysteries." (Recall here that the word *mysteries* does not mean what is unknown, but what is so profound and significant that it cannot but be described as the "sacred mysteries" of Christ's love poured out for us, which we experience through the rites of the liturgy.)

Now the origin of this period of continuing formation was the fourth century, when bishops would instruct the newly initiated about what had occurred to them at the Easter Vigil. One example of these "mystagogic catecheses" is from St. Cyril, ordained bishop in Jerusalem in the fourth century (actually about 351). During Lent, he met frequently with those to be baptized and instructed them in the faith (these are called "catecheses" or "catechetical lectures"). He then met every day during the Easter octave to explain the meaning of the sacred mysteries of initiation. The last two lectures concern the Eucharist. The first of these explains how the Eucharist is food for immortality; the second describes the meaning of what occurs in the rites and gestures of the Mass. For Cyril, the dominant image is that the Eucharist is a sacred *meal* and what the faithful and the newly initiated receive is *food* for the journey of life. In the second of these catecheses, which concerns how to receive Communion, Cyril explains that they receive it in their hand precisely because it is food and we take it as we take other foods. Then he tells them that when they approach to receive from now on, they are to make their left hand a kind of throne for their right hand so that they can receive the eucharistic bread in the palm of their right hands and then say "Amen" as they receive it. After they consume the bread, they are to approach to receive the eucharistic cup and say "Amen" to what they receive, the "cup of His Blood."

This combination of directives of how to receive Communion reflected the predominant theology of the Eucharist at the time—that it was the meal for the pilgrim church's journey to the kingdom of heaven. In Cyril's theology, the eucharistic action was the central *image* and *foretaste* of the fullness of experiencing the risen Lord, which will occur only in the kingdom of heaven in eternity. Hence, he understands that the Eucharist is central, but provisional: a real presence, but a presence that is promissory of the full reality of experiencing the whole exalted Christ in eternity.

By the ninth century, the context of explaining what the Eucharist is and how to receive it changed. Part of this had to do with the way people then could comprehend what was real and what was not real. Succinctly put, the agenda now was to explain what the eucharistic species itself was. It was no longer to explain what the whole rite of the Mass (Gathering, Word, Eucharistic Prayer, Communion, Dismissal) meant theologically and spiritually. What happened from the ninth century on was a shift to an emphasis on what the eucharistic species was and on increased reverence for the species as the place of the real presence of Christ himself. This was also the time when the church came to emphasize the moment of consecration at the words "This is my body...blood." It is not a surprise, therefore, that at this time theologians and bishops would emphasize the uniqueness of Christ's presence in bread and wine and that when the laity did receive Communion (which became more and more infrequent), they were not to touch the species itself but should extend their tongues as an act of reverence.

Now before we choose one period over another, it should be recalled here that both periods and examples emphasized the theology of the Eucharist as food sustaining us as the pilgrim church. The food that Cyril described so profoundly in the fourth century came to be appreciated in the Middle Ages as one of the medicines that we need to help heal and cure us as we journey to the kingdom of heaven. What also occurred was a clear shift of emphasis to the act of consecration and the (rare) act of receiving Communion. The customary gesture during the Eucharistic Prayer was now kneeling; the customary way to receive was on the tongue.

What has occurred after the Vatican II–reform of the Mass has been an appropriate reemphasis on the Eucharist as food and on the Eucharistic Prayer as our solemn proclamation of thanksgiving, which we now hear prayed aloud and in which we participate by acclamations. These emphases in the rite have led many conferences of bishops to request that people be allowed to have the option of receiving Communion in the hand, which gesture would ratify these renewed emphases in the Liturgy of the Mass and in the theology of the Eucharist today.

I suspect this is a long way of answering your question by saying that either gesture may be chosen today and that the return of the opportunity to receive in the hand demonstrates a renewed appreciation of the Eucharist as the food of immortality, to "take and eat" as we take and other foods. However, it is also important to recall that, whatever manner of receiving Communion is chosen, the way we receive should be marked with signs of reverence and devotion. There should be nothing casual about receiving the Eucharist. Therefore, we profit by examining how well we extend the palm of our hands to the eucharistic minister, how reverently we take the Eucharist, and with what conviction and commitment we say "Amen" to the declaration "Body of Christ."

77. Is it true that in the extraordinary form of the Mass the priest says a much longer prayer when communicants receive than "the body...blood of Christ" and we respond, "Amen"? Can you explain?

You are quite right that the prayer the priest uses in the extraordinary form is longer. It also does not require a response. (What may be of interest here is that when I checked the Latin edition of the Tridentine Missal used by the priest at the altar, I found no directions about the manner of distributing Communion. But in one of the Tridentine "hand missals" used by the faithful, I did find the directives for distribution. Even here, however, what is notable is that there is a red line across the page at the beginning and end of this section, indicating that this was not part of every Mass, just when laypeople would receive Communion. Might one legitimately conjecture that the directives for the Tridentine Mass concern only what the priest did and that Communion distribution was considered at least "something else"?).

What is clear is that in the Tridentine Missal, before he received Communion, the priest said to himself in Latin, "May the body of our Lord Jesus Christ preserve my soul for everlasting life. Amen." He changed the text slightly as he received from the chalice: "May the blood...." Then when he distributed Communion (under the species of the bread only), he said this same prayer as he gave each communicant the host on the tongue; he simply changed the pronoun to say (again in Latin), "preserve *your* soul...." The only bit of personal recollection I can add from pre–Vatican II is that, as an altar server who held the paten under the chin of those receiving Communion, I noticed that the priest did not always say this whole text for each communicant. I suspect that as people started to receive Communion more and more frequently and regularly, their numbers grew, and priests judged that Communion would take too much time if they said this longer prayer over each person receiving.

The present instruction in the ordinary form of the Mass states that the minister says, "Body of Christ," and the communicant responds, "Amen." This returns to a practice that is amply documented in the patristic era, specifically by St. Augustine. The *Catechism of the Catholic Church* cites his text in full (n. 1396) from one of his sermons (number 272), where he describes what occurs at Communion. He emphasizes who we are who come to receive: members of Christ. Hence, what we receive is really who we are—the Body of Christ. Therefore, he exhorts us to say, "Amen" (meaning, "Yes, it is true") to the Eucharist, and to live as a member of the Body of Christ. What we have here is another example of what I referred to before as the *multivalence* (many meanings) of liturgical texts. One meaning concerns our assent in faith to the Eucharist as Christ's body; but another level concerns our assent to living with one another as members of Christ's Body. From what we have been saying throughout much of this book, what we have here is not surprising—namely, an emphasis on the church, the community with whom we celebrate Mass, and not just on the eucharistic species. Recalling the actual text of the Tridentine Rite, you will notice that it emphasized individual salvation ("preserve my/your soul"). The return in the new Missal to "Body of Christ" requires not only a verbal response, "Amen," but a commitment to living with one another as members of Christ.

78. Why is it that sometimes only the priest and those at the altar receive from the chalice? Why not the whole congregation? Are there regulations about when the laity can receive from the chalice?

If you experience a Mass when only the priest and those at the altar receive from the chalice, this is either because of custom or because a particular bishop has prohibited the distribution under both species on Sundays. But perhaps I'm getting ahead of myself. Once more, a little historical background and a review of current teaching can help here.

Certainly it has always been the custom that the priest received both the eucharistic bread and cup. Up through the twelfth century, the laity who received at all also customarily communicated from the chalice. As I have already noted when discussing the piety and practices about the Eucharist in the Middle Ages, certain shifts occurred, not the least of which involved the withholding of the chalice from the laity. Theologically the doctrine that was part of the reason that laity received less and less from the chalice was the doctrine of *concomitance*. This teaching (officially ratified by the church's magisterium in 1551 at the Council of Trent) was that Christ is totally present in both the eucharistic bread and the eucharistic wine. Hence, even if one received just one of the species, one received the whole, sacramental Christ.

The present *General Instruction of the Roman Missal* marks a dramatic shift away from the practice of restricting the chalice (but it does not teach anything at variance with the doctrine of concomitance). It states:

Holy Communion has a fuller form as a sign when it takes place under both kinds. For in this form the sign of the Eucharistic banquet is more clearly evident and clearer expression is given to the divine will by which the new and eternal Covenant is ratified in the Blood of the Lord, as also the connection between the Eucharistic banquet and the eschatological banquet in the Kingdom of the Father. (n. 281)

It goes on to stress that, when the eucharistic wine is so received, it better images the notion of the Eucharist as a banquet, and it indicates that this image of banquet is the better preparation for the "eschatological banquet" in the Father's kingdom that our present Eucharist anticipates and prepares for. The "sign value" described here is important. It recalls that Jesus' invitation at the Last Supper was *both* to take and eat, *as well as* to take and drink.

Because of the complexity (and delicacy) involved as to when Communion in both species is possible, allow me again to cite the *General Instruction of the Roman Missal*:

In addition to those cases given in the ritual books, Communion under both kinds is permitted for:

a) Priests who are not able to celebrate or concelebrate Mass;

b) the Deacon and others who perform some duty at the Mass;

c) members of communities at the conventual Mass or the "community" Mass, along with seminarians, and all those engaged in a retreat or taking part in a spiritual or pastoral gathering.

The diocesan Bishop may establish norms for Communion under both kinds for his own diocese, which are also to be observed in churches of religious and at celebrations with small groups. The diocesan Bishop is also given the

faculty to permit Communion under both kinds whenever it may seem appropriate to the Priest to whom a
community has been entrusted as its own shepherd, provided that the faithful have been well instructed and that
there is no danger of profanation of the Sacrament or of
the rite's becoming difficult because of the large number
of participants or for some other cause.

As to the manner of distributing Holy Communion
under both kinds to the faithful and the extent of the faculty for doing so, the Conferences of Bishops may publish
norms, once their decisions have received the recognitio
of the Apostolic See. (n. 283)

79. What does the church teach regarding the practice of intinction? Is it forbidden?

First of all so that all of us can be clear, *intinction* refers to the
practice of offering the laity a share in the eucharistic species by
dipping the consecrated bread into consecrated wine. This was first
documented in the West in seventh-century Spain and is found in
descriptions of the Mass through the era when the faithful no
longer received under two species. In the East, this has been a common practice since about the ninth century. When Communion is
distributed in this way in Eastern Rites, the eucharistic bread is a
cube-like shape and is leavened, and pieces are placed in the chalice for the priest to distribute to the faithful by a spoon.

As a means of communicating under two species, this practice was restored to the Western (Roman) Church in 1965. It is still
included in the *General Instruction of the Roman Missal* as one way
to distribute Communion (see nn. 191, 245, 287). In practice, however, if Communion is offered under two species, it is commonly
done by having everyone drink directly from the chalice (see n.
285). There are several reasons for this, but they derive principally
from the way the *General Instruction* describes the sign value of
Communion under both forms. Jesus said, "Take and eat…take and

drink." Hence, this admonition sanctions two parallel actions for sharing in the consecrated bread and wine—just as we take food and drink in parallel actions at mealtimes in daily life. The custom of "dunking" is very limited in our culture; some would suggest that it is not proper etiquette at all!

Furthermore, in pastoral practice, if intinction is *the* sole manner of receiving Communion, then we take away a person's legitimate right not to receive under both forms. This is especially problematic when recovering alcoholics want to receive Communion and the option of just one species is not offered to them. In addition, given the long-standing custom in the West that we use unleavened bread for the Eucharist, the use of wafer-thin bread makes it difficult to dip it into the chalice and distribute on the tongue. Issues of personal hygiene, saliva, and so on, come into play here in what can be characterized as providing at least potentially awkward circumstances and results.

For me, the issue of eucharistic symbolism and sign value comes into play very significantly. By this I mean that the Eucharist is a privileged sacramental and sacrificial meal and that whatever we can do to restore this to our experience of the Mass, the better. At its heart, what the church does in sacraments is to take what we normally do and use in human life and ritualize it for our public worship. Therefore, what we do at human meals—eat, drink, converse—is what we do at the Mass. We take bread and wine, bless them, and give them to the church for spiritual nourishment and sustenance. The better the sign value of taking, eating, and drinking in the Mass itself, the more faithful we are to what the Liturgy of the Mass implies and contains for eating *and* drinking.

80. Where does the extra consecrated bread and wine go?

The *General Instruction of the Roman Missal* (n. 163) states that after all have communicated, either the priest consumes the left-over hosts "or carries them to the place designated for the reservation of the Eucharist." This means the tabernacle, whether it is in a separate reservation chapel or in the church building itself.

The exact location of the tabernacle has been the subject of some controversy and no little discussion. The former edition of the *General Instruction* indicated that there should be a reservation chapel separate from the main body of the church. However, the revised *General Instruction* puts it this way:

> It is more appropriate as a sign that on an altar on which Mass is celebrated there not be a tabernacle in which the Most Holy Eucharist is reserved.
>
> Consequently, it is preferable that the tabernacle be located, according to the judgment of the diocesan Bishop:
>
> a) either in the sanctuary, apart from the altar of celebration, in an appropriate form and place, not excluding its being positioned on an old altar no longer used for celebration;
>
> b) or even in some chapel suitable for the private adoration and prayer of the faithful and organically connected to the church and readily noticeable by the Christian faithful. (n. 315)

Part of the sign value at work here that would justify having a separate reservation chapel is that the action of the Mass leads to the place of reservation and that the fitting act of adoration before the reserved Eucharist in the tabernacle is not the same thing as the liturgical action/event that occurs in and through the liturgy itself. Customarily, the tabernacle is a square or box-like vessel with a door and a key with a lock. The 2004 instruction *Redemptionis Sacramentum* from the Congregation for Divine Worship contains a helpful explanation of eucharistic reservation (see nn. 129–45).

The term *tabernacle* derives from the Latin *tabernaculum*, which means "tent." This term derives from the scriptures where the notion of God's dwelling in a tent with the chosen people is the basis for the pivotal text in the prologue of the Gospel of St. John: "The Word became flesh and dwelt among us" (John 1:14), where the verb *dwelt* derives from this term *tabernacle*—meaning that Jesus "pitched his tent" among us. Some historical perspective can help here. In the early church, the Eucharist was reserved primarily so that those who were sick, elderly, and so on—and thus could not celebrate the Mass with the community—could receive Communion from the reserved sacrament. Then, because the Eucharist was reserved, it became a legitimate object of adoration and devotion. This historical precedent helps us understand that even modern papal teaching about the reserved sacrament—for example, Pius XII's encyclical *Mediator Dei*, as well as *Redemptionis Sacramentum*, mentioned above—states that its primary rationale is for distribution to the sick, and that secondarily it becomes a proper object of devotion. In addition, given the circumstances of the increasing numbers of parishes not served by a priest and the frequency of having *Sunday Celebrations in the Absence of a Priest,* a third, quite new, rationale is so that there are hosts available for these services.

The architectural evidence we have of a place for reservation includes a variety of vessels suspended on a wire in the church (many of which were called a *pyx*), a "sacrament house," or a sacristy cupboard in which the eucharistic bread was kept. That the tabernacle became the most common location and was placed on an altar derives from a sixteenth-century custom that was eventually legislated in the nineteenth century for all churches.

Certainly one of the most pastorally effective practices since Vatican II has been the way deacons, acolytes, and eucharistic ministers have taken up the practice of bringing Communion to the sick after Sunday Mass. Sometimes such persons are dismissed from the Sunday assembly with the priest's blessing and the prayer of the community. When this is done on weekdays, the Eucharist is almost always taken from the tabernacle.

The *General Instruction of the Roman Missal* (n. 283) states that "any consecrated wine left over is consumed at the altar by the Priest or the Deacon or the duly instituted acolyte who ministered the chalice. The same then purifies, wipes, and arranges the sacred vessels in the usual way." Thus, there is no reservation of the precious blood of Christ.

81. Is the priest supposed to bring the consecrated hosts to the tabernacle? Must he clean the chalice at the altar after Communion?

The paragraph from the *General Instruction of the Roman Missal* cited above about what happens when the distribution of Communion has ended (n. 163) presumes that it is the priest himself who brings the leftover hosts to the place of reservation. In addition, the instruction *Redemptionis Sacramentum* states:

The Priest, once he has returned to the altar after the distribution of Communion, standing at the altar or at the credence table, purifies the paten or ciborium over the chalice, then purifies the chalice in accordance with the prescriptions of the Missal and wipes the chalice with the purificator. Where a Deacon is present, he returns with the Priest to the altar and purifies the vessels. It is permissible, however, especially if there are several vessels to be purified, to leave them, covered as may be appropriate, on a corporal on the altar or on the credence table, and for them to be purified by the Priest or Deacon immediately after Mass once the people have been dismissed. Moreover a duly instituted acolyte assists the Priest or Deacon in purifying and arranging the sacred vessels either at the altar or the credence table. In the absence of a Deacon, a duly instituted acolyte carries the sacred vessels to the credence table and there purifies, wipes and arranges them in the usual way. (n. 119)

My own sense here is that it is liturgically preferable to do the purifications at the credence table after Mass. Why? First, I think that just as the vessels are on the credence table before Mass and brought to the altar at the Preparation of the Gifts, so after Communion it is better to place them back on that table. Second, I think it best to take whatever time it would take to purify the vessels for silent prayer and thanksgiving after Communion. This is in accord with the Missal's directives that after Communion "the priest may return to the chair" and that "a period of silence may now be observed, or a psalm or song of praise may be sung." What I find important about this directive is that it emphasizes once more the value of periods of silence in the celebration of Mass and that if the priest returns to the chair (which I would regard as preferable), this would indicate a location separate from the altar where the concluding rites are more properly conducted.

82. What is the purpose of the Prayer after Communion? I seem to recall that sometimes it's about dismissal and other times about the hope of heaven.

Let me begin by recalling that word *multivalence* once again. What I want to suggest here is that, as we recall the principle that texts and parts of the Mass can have many meanings, what we should do to answer your question is to check what these texts themselves say and from this investigation to offer a summary insight about the nature of this prayer. I say this especially because the present Missal is very reticent about stating what themes this prayer should have. It simply states that the priest "prays for the fruits of the mystery just celebrated" (n. 89).

Among other things, sometimes this prayer refers to the hope of heaven (see the First Sunday of Advent), or living what we have celebrated (Christmas Mass at Midnight), or experiencing more fully the gift of salvation (Mary, Mother of God, January 1), or our response to the Eucharist by welcoming Christ in others (Baptism of the Lord). If I were asked for a brief explanation of the "theme" of this prayer, I would say that it most often refers to living out in daily life what we have celebrated and that it underscores how the Eucharist leads us to eternal life with God in the kingdom of heaven.

83. Why are the Rites after Communion so short?

The short answer is that they have a simple and direct purpose—to end the celebration and dismiss the community. The *General Instruction of the Roman Missal* says the following about these rites:

To the Concluding Rites belong the following:

a) brief announcements, should they be necessary;
b) the Priest's greeting and blessing, which on certain days and occasions is expanded and expressed by the Prayer over the People or another more solemn formula;
c) the dismissal of the people by the Deacon or the Priest, so that each may go back to doing good works, praising and blessing God;
d) the kissing of the altar by the Priest and the Deacon, followed by a profound bow to the altar by the Priest, the Deacon, and the other ministers. (n. 90)

Let's take a look at each of these.

First of all, the announcements *follow* the Prayer after Communion. The reasoning here is that the period of silence after receiving Communion should not be interrupted by parish announcements and then the prayer—I say this because I know of many parishes where this is the custom. I suspect the rationale is that the people are already seated after Communion, so why not do the announcements then. The more proper thing is to pray in silence, listen to the priest's prayer, and then have announcements. What is very interesting is that, in the documentation we have from the early church when deacons normally assisted at Mass, it was the deacons who gave the announcements. The reason was that because of his day-to-day ministry he would know who was sick or in need of the community's charity, or what community events were on the calendar. What is seemingly a "housekeeping" task really is meant to carry theological weight—namely, that altar and daily life are intrinsically connected.

The formula for the blessing itself may be as simple as "May almighty God bless you, the Father, and the Son, and the Holy Spirit." However, one of the features of the present Missal is the addition of twenty options for the threefold "solemn blessings" and some twenty-six options for a final Prayer over the People as part of the Concluding Rites. Since the priest may choose any of these at any time, I would suggest that a solemn blessing might best be used for Sundays of the seasons of Advent, Christmas, Lent, and Easter (the Missal provides blessings designed for these seasons) or for other solemn or special occasions. On less festive days, the priest might instead choose a Prayer over the People as part of the Concluding Rites. The only caution I might offer is that we should be attentive to how much of the Mass is spoken texts and that there should be a balance of speaking, singing, silence, and listening. To add another spoken prayer to a Mass with a lot of speaking might be to "overload" it and make it heavy with words.

84. I understand that Pope Benedict XVI added some options for the Dismissal at Mass. What are they and why did he do this?

During the Synod on the Eucharist in the Life and Mission of the Church the pope made the observation more than once that he judged there was not sufficient emphasis placed on living in daily life what we celebrate at Mass. In fact, the Latin *Ite missa est* (as I noted in answer to question 1) does contain elements of sending forth to live what we celebrate. But I think you will agree that the texts from the pope are more explicit:

Go and announce the Gospel of the Lord.

Go in peace, glorifying the Lord by your life.

VIII

Music at Mass

85. What kind of music is allowed at Mass?

Your question raises a number of issues, both theoretical and very practical. I'd say that no single feature of the revision of the Mass has had as much pastoral impact as has the reintroduction of popular participation at Mass through music. Allow me to offer three observations as I try to answer your important question: what Vatican II says about style, the procedure for implementing the liturgical reforms of Vatican II, and some of the governing principles for determining suitable music for Mass (from Vatican II and subsequent documents).

When discussing "sacred art and sacred furnishings" in general, the Liturgy Constitution states that "the Church has not adopted any particular style of art as its very own but has admitted styles from every period, according to the proper genius and circumstances of peoples and the requirements of the many different rites in the Church" (n. 123). This is a very important text because it respects variety in the styles of art that can and should be used in the liturgy, while at the same time it insists on the value of the use of arts in worship. I have spoken on a few occasions in this book about our using in worship things that are native to us as humans in our common worship of God. One of these is our talent to create things of beauty, which act of "creation" reflects the beauty, truth, and goodness of the living God. Our gifts for ingenuity and artistic creativity are always brought to bear in the act of worship. Both Pope John Paul II (especially in his "Letter to Artists") and Pope Benedict XVI have noted the importance of beauty in the liturgy and aesthetics in general. Over the course of the centuries in our Catholic tradition, these gifts have been used in varied and different ways, depending, among other things, on the needs of the liturgy at the time and the culture of the time. It is for this reason, primarily, that this same Liturgy Constitution insists that bishops of different countries oversee how the arts are utilized in worship (n. 127) and adapt what the Constitution says "to the needs and customs of their different regions" (n. 128).

What has therefore occurred in the United States (and in other countries, respectively) has been the publication of documents to specify the way the general teachings of the church about music can and should be implemented. Almost immediately after the reform of the liturgy, the United States Bishops' Conference issued *Music in Catholic Worship* (1972), which was principally about the Mass. A decade later, the conference published *Liturgical Music Today* (1982), which is principally about the other sacraments and the Hours. These two documents served for a generation to guide and support popular participation in the liturgy through music. It was with the publication of the Fifth Instruction on the Implementation of the Liturgy, *Liturgiam Authenticam* (2001), that the issue of evaluating these documents and offering additional guidance on liturgical music was considered. In fact, *Liturgiam Authenticam* itself asked that the national bishops' conferences should draw up a directory or repertory of appropriate liturgical texts intended for liturgical singing (n. 108). The music subcommittee of the USCCB Committee on Divine Worship set about a series of national consultations about liturgical music and then charged a drafting committee with the responsibility of writing a draft of such a document that would, in effect, replace *Music in Catholic Worship*. Throughout these "implementation" documents, we find great respect paid to the variety of expression within the cultural diversity of the United States (for example, African American, Latino, and other ethnic groups) at the very same time that the statements point to the value of making three "judgments" about the suitability of music at liturgy:

> *A musical judgment*: is it of good musical quality?
>
> *A liturgical judgment*: does it serve the needs of the reformed liturgy?
>
> *A pastoral judgment*: does it serve the assembly that gathers for worship?

These three judgments should come together and enable those choosing the music to come up with one evaluation about what is appropriate for the liturgy (see *Sing to the Lord*, nn. 126–36).

The liturgical judgment just mentioned leads me to the issue of principles about what is suitable for liturgical music today. It is clear from the Liturgy Constitution—through the documents governing the reform of the liturgy from Rome, plus the specifications of the individual rites themselves—that above all the key to appropriate music at liturgy is that it be *music that serves the liturgy*. A basic premise throughout all the reform documents is that the texts of the liturgy that should be sung should be set to music that all those who participate can sing. By no means does this mean that the music should be pedestrian or of low quality—in fact, just the opposite is asked for in the "musical judgment" cited above! What is at stake is the congregation's active participation at Mass. They should not be passive or silent but should participate through singing as much as possible.

Sometimes the question of style interfaces with the question of what is appropriate for liturgy, and then sides can be drawn with people coming down on either side. An optimal music style (or styles) would be one that reflects and respects the variety of persons and cultures that comprise the gathered assembly at Mass, and is written to suit the needs of the reformed Mass itself. I suspect that precisely because this is such a tall order, we may well find ourselves disappointed when the music we use at Mass is wanting. We have a way to go in composing more adequate music for liturgical participation—this remains an agenda for us. But remembering how far we have come should be a cause of optimism and hope. My own sense is that we are in a maturation period in this area, and that some of the music that was published almost immediately after the reform of the Mass has indeed been judged trite and is simply not used anymore.

86. What parts of the Mass should be sung?

Your question is very well phrased because it asks what parts *of the Mass* should be sung, indicating precisely the chief aim in the present reform of liturgical music—that the important texts *of the Mass* be sung before any other music is added to the liturgy. Taking my lead from what I have already indicated about the relative importance of different parts of the Mass—specifically, how important the proclamation of the Eucharistic Prayer is for the Mass—and in light of the revised Order of Mass as well as the American document *Sing to the Lord*, I will indicate the weight to be given to various parts of the Mass. The order that follows is from *Sing to the Lord* (n. 115). It begins with the most important category and ends with the least important.

Dialogues and Acclamations. Dialogues engage priest, deacon, and lector with the gathered assembly because they bring about communion among them (see *General Instruction of the Roman Missal*, nn. 34 and 40). Dialogues include such texts as "God, come to my assistance," "The Lord be with you," and so on. The acclamations are the Gospel Acclamation, the *Sanctus*, the Mystery of Faith, and the Great Amen. The rationale here is that these acclamations are intrinsic to the Mass and singing them indicates the great importance that these parts have. This is especially true of the acclamations that are intrinsic to the Eucharistic Prayer (see response to question 59).

Antiphons and Psalms. The psalms are meant to be sung whenever possible. The Responsorial Psalm is an intrinsic part of the Liturgy of the Word. The Entrance (formerly called the *Introit*) and Communion songs are important to accompany the ritual actions of movement during the Mass itself. (See my answer to question 28 about what music is appropriate at the Entrance and Communion processions.) The Responsorial Psalm is the sung response (almost always from the psalms) to the first reading. Singing the response helps to draw out the meaning of the psalm as it relates to this particular reading. As a kind of "musical echo," the psalm response balances the act of proclamation with prayerful personal appropriation of the text through the psalm.

Refrains and Repeated Responses. These include the *Kyrie* and *Agnus Dei* and the response to the Prayer of the Faithful at Mass.

Ordinary Chants. In the Tridentine Missal we used the terms *ordinary* and *proper* of the Mass. The ordinary referred to the fixed texts; the proper chants were those that changed because of the feast or season. In the present terminology, ordinary chants refer to the Lord, Have Mercy, as well as to the Glory to God, Lord's Prayer, Lamb of God, and Profession of Faith. Even here there is a kind of hierarchy since the Lamb of God (which accompanies the action of breaking the bread receives greater emphasis than the Profession of Faith (the recitation of which stands on its own as a liturgical "action"). You will notice a lot of variety here, since not every Mass includes a sung Lord, Have Mercy (other forms of the Penitential Rite may be used) and since the Glory to God is not part of the daily Mass structure (except for special feasts).

Hymns. The clearest example of a hymn in the structure of the Mass itself is the *Gloria.* Other hymns may be sung at other parts of the Mass, for example, at the Entrance, Preparation of the Gifts, Communion, and Recessional. *Sing to the Lord* (n. 115 d) asserts that in accord with the uninterrupted practice of five centuries, nothing prevents the use of some congregational hymns coming from other Christian traditions, provided that they reflect Catholic teaching and are appropriate to the Catholic liturgy.

87. What is the proper role of liturgical music in the Mass?

Succinctly put, I'd say that the role of music is to enhance the liturgy as a sung and enacted ritual and that the more the music supports the act of worship in the Mass, the better.

I can remember some of the early debates about the reform of music in the liturgy. The earliest descriptions called for music that itself was liturgical, meaning that it served the rites and the texts, rather than music that was simply *at* the liturgy, meaning hymns or other music commonly in vogue added on to the Mass. More recently I think that a better phrase is *musical liturgy.* This phrase immediately connotes that music is intrinsic to liturgy and that by its nature a generous amount of the liturgy's texts should be sung. The more the nature of the Mass as *musical liturgy* can be appreciated through the wise choice of types of music that can be sung, the better off we are in sustaining the kind of integral vision of music and liturgy that the documents about the revised liturgy presume. The term often heard today is *ritual music*, which, I think, tries to capture this sense of *musical liturgy*. In addition, I would also say that a judicious use of music can enhance the liturgical experience of festivity and celebration and that this is always an ongoing task because of the nature of the reformed Mass.

The principle enunciated in the *General Instruction of the Liturgy of the Hours* about *progressive solemnity* is operative here. The term *progressive solemnity* suggests that given the number of legitimate options for singing in the Mass (and among the various roles of who does the singing: congregation, cantor, choir, schola, or others), a careful selection from these options can enhance the solemnity of certain celebrations while it also characterizes other occasions as less festive. For example, one might want to enhance the liturgies of the Sundays of the Easter season by emphasizing the singing of the eucharistic acclamations and the Glory to God with particularly robust and festive music, but during the Lenten Sundays an atmosphere of simplicity and directness could be achieved by minimizing the complexity of the music chosen and sung. In fact, some parishes that wish to move away from emphasizing the recessional song (because it is not an intrinsic part *of the Mass*) have chosen Lent as a season when they have no music after the deacon's (or priest's) dismissal. What progressive solemnity offers is a way to choose from a number of options in the Mass and to invite the creativity and artistry of musicians that can continue to enhance the kind of participation that the reformed liturgy presumes.

88. Is any "religious" song okay to sing at a Mass? If not, where do the songs come from? Who picks them?

No, not every "religious" song is all right for the Mass. Part of the reason is that the emphasis is now placed on singing the texts *of the Mass* itself, and additional music that reflects Catholic teach-

ing and Catholic liturgical practice. But this does not mean that
there is no room for variety and creativity. There are countless
musical resources available from a good number of musical pub-
lishing houses. Part of the challenge of good liturgical planning is
to sort through the "tried and true" and the "new and different"
and to work toward theologically and liturgically sound, as well as
aesthetically pleasing, experiences of music at Mass.

At this point of the ongoing implementation of the reformed
liturgy, I would like to give special emphasis to the singing of the
psalms (as already cited in the answer to question 86). The Book of
Psalms itself is the church's prayer book in the liturgy, and the more
we can use these texts in the Mass, the better off we are to help
people rediscover the depth, complexity, and richness of these
prayers. In addition, if psalms are chosen to be sung as processional
chants, this opens up the possibility of having the congregation
join in the antiphon while the cantor, schola, or choir sings the
requisite number of verses of the psalm to accompany the procession. This option might better facilitate the people's participation
in singing at Communion, because if they sing only the antiphons
they will not need to carry worship aids or worship books in procession, which makes the act of receiving the Eucharist in the hand
and from the chalice at least somewhat cumbersome.

Now as to who chooses the music, that's a good but complex
question! A lot depends on the structure your parish has for *planning* the whole Mass. Unlike the extraordinary form of the Mass,
the present Missal offers a number of options in the liturgy that
need to be chosen carefully in order that the Mass be conducted in
a reverent manner that invites familiarity with its parts for the sake
of popular participation. Some of these include choosing the
Penitential Rite, Preface, Eucharistic Prayer, Blessing, Dismissal, and
more, or composing the General Intercessions or the announcements at the end of Mass. When these choices have been made,
there is the question of what parts of these are to be sung, as well as
the larger issue of what musical settings for the acclamations and
other sung texts are appropriate. Finally, there is the question of

what texts and music will be sung that supplement or take the place of what is in the Missal (for example, procession songs). Ideally there should be some group process at work to choose the various parts of the Mass, including significant musical input from those charged with the parish's musical ministry. So to the precise question of "who decides," I'd have to say "it depends," but it should not be arbitrary or left only to those who are trained musicians. The issue is no longer to "pick the hymns" but to choose options wisely, both textual and musical, that can enhance what we celebrate at Mass.

89. What about Latin and Gregorian chant? Can or should we still sing them?

Thank you for a question that serves as a way of describing some features of the implementation of both the extraordinary form of the Mass and the ordinary form. The issue of the value and use of Gregorian chant goes back to the document from Pope Pius X in 1903, *Tra le Sollecutidini,* in which he took bold leadership in the direction that led ultimately to the kind of reform of the liturgy that stresses popular participation so much. In fact, what Pope Pius X called for in restoring the "patrimony of Gregorian chant" for use in the Mass was precisely that—so that the people could take part in the (then extraordinary form of the) Mass through singing the chant melodies that were simpler than much of the polyphony sung by choirs at the time. To make my point a bit clearer, may I return to the answers to questions 85 and 86, where I distinguished the issue of appropriate *musical style* from the *ritual requirements of the Mass.* I would also like to reiterate what I suggested there, namely, that the church has never adopted any one style of art (architecture, music, and so on) as its own, but has encouraged many and different kinds of musical styles to be used in the liturgy.

Now given the present emphasis on popular participation in the liturgy itself, what Pius X had to say about restoring chant is quite applicable, in terms both of how it meets the liturgical need of fostering participation and how it addresses the issue of a desirable style of music. One of the great features of the simple chant style is that it fosters participation even by those untrained in music. Its simplicity made it a desirable way to participate musically in the Latin Mass. Now that the Mass is in the vernacular, the same kind of simple and direct *style* of music would be highly desirable. Whether this means that we sing Gregorian chant as a regular part of the liturgy in our parishes is another matter.

Clearly one of the advantages of singing Gregorian chant is its universality—these same melodies can be sung throughout the world. Therefore, given the amount of travel that people do today, there is clearly something to be said in favor of retaining some chant pieces so that when traveling and participating in liturgy not in our native language, then at least these parts can serve as familiar vehicles for participation. In addition, some recent instructions from Rome about music support the preservation of this body of music as an important cultural and liturgical contribution of the Catholic Church. Therefore, one pastoral application of what I have been saying might be to sing the chant as one or another of the ordinary chants of the Mass on a somewhat regular basis, for example, the *Sanctus, Agnus Dei*, and so on. This would afford the sense of universality along with the value of participation through what is simple and direct, both textually and musically.

But I would also like to use this argument about style and the demands of the ordinary form of the Mass to offer a challenge to contemporary composers of liturgical music. It seems that we have established some sense of familiarity in liturgical participation through music with the rather common use of some settings to the acclamations for the Eucharistic Prayer, the Alleluia, and so on. What I think remains an important unfinished agenda item is the composition of a similar kind of familiar (American idiom?) music for the processional chants at the Entrance and Communion, based on the psalms. While we have, I think, made significant progress in deepening our participation in and appreciation of the Responsorial Psalm, I also think that a good bit of work remains to be done on these processional chants. Now what I am not saying is that we should do this in order to make this music standard or required (as parts of the chant are required in the extraordinary form of the Mass). What I am arguing for is another vehicle whereby congregations can participate in the Mass by singing psalms set to music that reflects the simplicity, directness, and depth of the Gregorian chant.

A last thought. Sometimes the corpus of Gregorian chant is exalted as the "be all and end all"—and its music *is* rather fine. But I'd like to offer the thought that it took a long time for a lot of other chant texts to find their way to the scriptorium's floor in the monasteries that reproduced them before the "final" chant book was produced! Trial and error marked the development of that style of sung prayer. It is my assessment that with continued patience and effort we will continue to move toward developing a fine repertoire of music for the Mass. But this takes a great deal of time.

IX

Eucharistic Doctrine
and Discipline

90. I was taught that the "real presence" was in the consecrated bread and wine, but today I keep hearing about Christ being present in other things, such as the scriptures, the assembly, and the priest. Can you clarify this for me?

You are quite right about what you were taught, that Christ's "real presence" is in the consecrated bread and wine. But what you are hearing today about Christ being present in many ways is also true. Let's take a theoretical and historical step backward to explain. It may sound a little harsh at first, but when it comes to the church's defined teaching about sacraments throughout its history, what is clear is that the body of that teaching is relatively small and that it has largely been reactive to errors. This is to say that when the church faced controversies about the understanding of what the Eucharist was, it then tried to clear up errors and misunderstandings by asserting truths about the Eucharist that were clear and precise answers to the errors of the time. Specifically, this means that as the church evolved through the Middle Ages, the term *real presence* came about as a helpful way to assert that Christ was present in the consecrated bread and wine. The controversy that required this definition centered around one Berengarius of Tours (France) in the eleventh century. Later on, when debates about Christ's presence in the Eucharist were renewed in the controversies with the Reformers in the sixteenth century (Luther, Calvin, Zwingli, and others), the issues were slightly different and the church found itself required to defend the real presence by using the term *transubstantiation*. This particular term comes from the Aristotelian philosophy that distinguishes between the reality of a thing and what it looks like, or—to use the precise Aristotelian language—between a thing's *substance* and its *accidents*. At the consecration, the *substance* of the bread and wine is changed into the *substance* of the body and blood of Christ. But the *accidents* of the bread and wine—what we see and taste at Communion—remain the same.

The *Decree on the Holy Eucharist* from the Council of Trent (sixteenth century), which responded to the Reformers' teachings, contains eight chapters, the first of which is entitled "The Real Presence of Our Lord Jesus Christ in the Most Holy Sacrament of the Eucharist." It is here that we find the phrase that Christ is present *truly, really, and substantially* in the consecrated bread. Later, in chapter 4, the decree also asserts that *transubstantiation* is "a most fitting way" (the Latin word is *aptissime*) to describe the change of bread and wine into the body and blood of Christ. The church has relied on these terms for centuries to ensure orthodox belief.

At Vatican II, however, because the polemics of the Reformation were no longer the issue at hand, it was judged best to reemphasize other ways in which Christ is present in the Eucharist, none of which were ever denied by the church but had suffered neglect because of the legitimate emphasis on Christ's presence in the bread and wine. In other words, the church once more had the opportunity to reinvent its teaching in light of present theological and pastoral need. So, in the Liturgy Constitution of Vatican II, it states that "in the sacrifice of the Mass" Christ is present "not only in the person of his minister, but especially in the eucharistic elements…[and that] he is present in his word [and] lastly when the Church prays and sings" (n. 7). This is a significant statement, for it refocuses our attention on these other, very traditional ways in which Christ is present to us in the Eucharist. Pope Paul VI reiterated this teaching in his encyclical *Mysterium Fidei* (1965) when he states that "the *real presence* [should] not exclude the other kinds as though they were not real, but because it is real par excellence, since it is substantial, in the sense that Christ whole and entire, God and man, becomes present" (n. 39). These statements are summarized in the document from the Vatican's Congregation of Rites in 1965 (*Eucharisticum Mysterium*) when it speaks about the *modes* of Christ's presence: in the assembly of the faithful, in his word, in the person of the minister, and "above all in the eucharistic elements" (n. 9). Now, you may ask, why does the mode of Christ in the elements still seem to receive greater emphasis? Well, the fact remains that Catholic doctrine, precisely defined at Trent, did place great emphasis on Christ's presence in the eucharistic elements of bread and wine, and this should not be lost in contemporary descriptions. The way the church's liturgical texts describe Christ's presence is in the *General Instruction to the Roman Missal* (n. 28) where it states, "Christ is really present in the very assembly gathered in his name, in the person of the minister, in his word, and indeed substantially and uninterruptedly under the Eucharistic species."

If I were to try to summarize the church's teaching, I'd say that Christ is present in the Eucharist, and in trying to explain the *ways* he is present to the church, I'd emphasize four ways: assembly, Word, species, and minister. I find the word *mode* to be very useful in explaining Christ's presence because it emphasizes *that Christ himself is present in various ways.* A good human analogy may be how we humans are "present" to each other—through words, gestures, and signs of relationship or affection. Just as we use words and gestures to express our relationship to each other so it is through the Liturgy of the Eucharist that the church uses words, gestures, and signs to communicate the one presence of Christ with us in varied ways. Christ is present where "two or three are gathered in [his] name" (Matt 18:20), through the spoken speech of the proclaimed scriptures, through the action of the transformation and communion in the bread and wine become the body and blood of Christ, and through the ordained minister acting in the very person of Christ. Through all of this discussion, we realize that Christ's intimate and personal commitment to the church is realized and expressed through the whole Liturgy of the Eucharist.

91. Is it true that in a survey of American Catholics, most said that they did not believe that at Mass the bread and wine are changed into the body and blood of Christ?

As I have thought about framing an answer to your question, I realized that I was thinking like a theologian but that I would likely sound like a lawyer when I answered it! I say this because I think lawyers are noted for care with words and language, and your question requires that I be very careful about the language used in the survey and the summary results that have been popularized. I will discuss a few surveys about the Eucharist. The first, now almost twenty years old, gained immediate notoriety. In late May and early June 1994, Peter Steinfels edited a four-part series of articles in the *New York Times* about the Catholic Church in America. In the last of the articles (June 1, 1994), he summarized the results of a *New York Times / CBS News* poll, which in fact was subtitled "American Catholics: A Church Divided." It is important to examine the exact wording of the question and proposed answers you ask about. The text of the survey asked: "At the Mass, are the bread and wine changed into the body and blood of Christ," or are they "symbolic reminders of Christ"?

What concerns me (and others, such as the late Cardinal Avery Dulles) is the way this issue was framed. When you put the terms *change* and *symbolic reminders* in opposition, I think you are separating what in our theological tradition are really inseparable. For example, throughout this book I have been careful to use the word *memorial* and the command "Do this in memory of me" in a positive way. I have also indicated that, for a good part of our tradition on eucharistic teaching, the terms *symbol* and *sign* have been very important. When the church uses them, it is essentially to make sure that the presence of Christ in the Eucharist is understood to be qualitatively different from the normal, physical notion of presence and the words we use to describe that kind of presence. In effect, the church's teaching about the Eucharist from as far back as St. Augustine was and is always couched in sacramental and "sign" language. Therefore, when I read that in this poll one had to choose between the word *change* and the very useful terms *symbolic* and *reminders*, then I questioned the usefulness of the poll itself. As it stands, I would have chosen the first answer—"changed into the body and blood"—but I really would have preferred a different set of choices. (If I sound like a lawyer parsing words, remember that I warned you!)

Now a second part to your question concerns what percentage said what, and whether it was a majority. The poll was broken down into age categories that ranged from 18 to 65 and older. In summary, the younger the group, the less likely they were to choose that the bread and wine are "changed into the body and blood of Christ" (30 percent of the youngest poll-takers versus 51 percent of the oldest).

I'd say we should do two things with these figures. First, we should take this poll at face value and realize its language was flawed because it separated *change* from *symbol* and/or *memorial*, which to my mind cannot be separated. Second, we should make sure that, when appropriate through the range of education programs and opportunities, we emphasize the active and real modes of the presence*s* of Christ (as described in the previous answer) so that we can firmly reiterate the fullness of Catholic teaching about the presence of Christ at Mass.

Data from a 2001 poll about eucharistic belief among those between the ages of 20 and 39 is summarized in the book *Young Adult Catholics* (edited by Dean Hoge, William Dinges, Mary Johnson, and Juan Gonzalez). It reveals a particularly strong fascination in this age group for sacramentality as a chief characteristic of Roman Catholicism. This poll asserts that the chief characteristics of Catholicism are not diminished among these young adults, even though the ability to articulate what they mean (for example, the doctrine of the real presence) is sometimes unclear or unfocused. The authors observe that "regarding the distinctive Catholic understanding of the Mass, our sample [of respondents] have a stronger belief in the real presence than indicated in other polls." In fact, of those surveyed, 87 percent of non-Latinos and 96 percent of the Latinos agreed with the statement that "in the Mass the bread and wine actually become the body and blood of Christ." In addition, what is of interest is that what was positive about their experience of liturgy was homilies, music, and a vibrant sense of community. They rated the liturgy negatively when it was "boring," "mechanical," or "unwelcoming."

Clearly, what is important is the way polls are worded. In his evaluation of the polls conducted about the Eucharist in the past decade, James Davidson, a sociologist of religious trends, argues that results are better (that is, more able to be interpreted as an accurate reflection of what people actually believe) when respondents are provided with succinct responses that are theologically precise and accurate. He offers two hypotheses: that there has been some decline about belief in the real presence of Christ in the Eucharist, but that, despite this, the most recent research shows that a majority of Catholics still agree with the church's teaching that the bread and wine actually become the body and blood of Christ. A majority also believe that the real presence is closer to the core of the Catholic faith than many other church teachings.

Finally, recent polls on what American Catholics believe, as reported in 2008 and again in 2011 by the Center for Applied Research in the Apostolate, indicate that belief in the real presence and the importance of belonging to a church that celebrates the sacraments, especially the Mass, still score among the highest possible answers to the questions asked.

And again, the way surveys are worded matters a great deal.

92. What makes our teaching on the Eucharist different from that of other churches?

I suspect that I might have had an easier job of answering your probing question before Vatican II, rather than now! I say this because much of our Catholic doctrine on the Eucharist was determined because of the controversies at the time of the Reformation. The language of the Council of Trent was definitive and often described Catholic teaching over against what others taught. In fact, much of the language of the decrees of Trent stated, "If anyone teaches [a named error], let him/her be condemned." In their legitimate concern to support traditional Catholic teaching, the bishops at Trent took positions that were often diametrically opposed to those of the Reformers about such things as the Eucharist as sacrifice, Communion under two species, and more.

Because Martin Luther firmly taught that the Eucharist was a gift from God (a *beneficium*), it could not be a sacrifice (*sacrificium*). This led the council fathers at Trent to state explicitly and fully that the Eucharist was indeed a sacrifice (session 22, September 1562, canons 1738–60). Similarly, when the bishops at Trent faced the reformers' insistence that one had to receive both the eucharistic bread and cup at Mass, they turned to the commonly held doctrine of *concomitance*. This doctrine, which teaches that one could receive Christ by partaking of the eucharistic bread only, was thus asserted at Trent (session 21, July 1562, canons 1725–34).

After the Council of Trent, the church issued *The Catechism of the Council of Trent*, summarizing its chief teachings in a useful question-and-answer format. This led to the eventual publication of American versions of the catechism (called *The Baltimore Catechism*) for use in educational programs in America. Therefore, what American Catholics were commonly taught before Vatican II was a set of teachings asserting our beliefs over against those of the reformers (most often grouped together as "Protestants"). So it is not surprising that Catholics asserted their belief in Christ's real presence in the Mass, that they called the change in bread and wine *transubstantiation*, that they said the Eucharist was indeed a sacrifice, and that they believed one need receive only the species of the eucharistic bread, not both bread and cup, to receive Christ.

At Vatican II, the church sought to reemphasize its core teachings in a more pastoral, invitational way and strove to distinguish what we held to as Catholic beliefs from what *seemed* to be a part of that core set of beliefs: in other words, to separate *what* we believed from *the way it was expressed*. Since Vatican II, there has been a reemphasis on the fourfold presence of Christ at Mass, not just language about the real presence in the eucharistic species of consecrated bread and wine. Also, Vatican II marked the beginning of a reemphasis on the power and efficaciousness of Christ's presence through the proclaimed word, which was certainly something we Catholics shied away from after Trent. Also, given the increased opportunities that we Catholics have today to receive both species, our traditional doctrine of concomitance, while not changed or revised, remains in place but is certainly not emphasized as it was after Trent.

In addition, given the ecumenical climate ushered in at Vatican II, there is a whole new way of looking at issues about the Mass, not just in terms of what "we" teach and what "they" teach, but what we can affirm together and what we need to dialogue about more fully. This leads me not only to think in terms of what makes our teaching about the Eucharist different from other churches, but also to realize that sometimes today what we are dealing with are *degrees of difference*. Hence, for example, as Catholics we assert that the Eucharist is a sacrifice, the same sacrifice of Jesus at Calvary. Today most churches dating from the Reformation teach that to some degree at least, the Eucharist is the sacrifice of Jesus. What makes our teachings different today on this issue is a matter of degree. Similarly, when it comes to asserting our belief in the real presence of Christ in the Eucharist, we Catholics have traditionally used the term *transubstantiation*, but today we are also able to use other terms. (Recall what I said regarding the assertion in the Vatican document *Eucharisticum Mysterium* that, provided we sustain the meaning of the term *transubstantiation*, we can develop new terminology to describe the Eucharist that contemporary Catholics may find easier to comprehend.) Many Protestants never liked this term because it was unbiblical, and yet some eventually used *consubstantiation* (meaning that Christ was present *with* the bread and wine) to distinguish their teaching from ours. Today I'd say that the vast majority of the Christian churches prefer the biblical language "This is my body...blood," and much Catholic teaching today uses the same phrasing.

Does this mean that we all now believe the same things about the Eucharist? No. But it does mean that we need to be very careful and exacting when we describe what we believe and the way it is phrased. It also means that we Catholics have some practices that are not shared by other churches, such as acts of reverence to the Eucharist during the liturgy and when the eucharistic bread is reserved after Mass. The current ecumenical climate also has helped us to restore practices that were never condemned but that seemed to be "non-Catholic," such as Mass in the vernacular, people participating in the whole Mass, and the Eucharist given under two species. We Catholics have regained this territory that Protestants never surrendered at the Reformation.

Allow me to say at least a word about how we Catholics have gained insight into eucharistic teaching from the Eastern Churches. Their emphasis on the role of the Holy Spirit in all liturgy and their emphasis on the invocation of the Holy Spirit through the prayer called the Epiclesis has helped us Catholics reemphasize the way the Spirit acts in our liturgy. From Trent on, this was a silent part of our traditional teaching. The revived epicletic prayers in much of the revised liturgy have helped us to readdress this neglected but nonetheless very traditional and important part of our liturgy and theology.

93. How can the real presence of our Lord continue in the bread and wine after the eucharistic celebration has ended?

I suspect that there are a number of ways of answering your intriguing question. But allow me to offer two approaches, one philosophical and the other in light of the church's practice. I call the first part of this answer "philosophical" because it has to do with what is real as a result of human actions and speech. When the priest prays the Eucharistic Prayer—especially when he invokes the Holy Spirit in the Epiclesis and uses the words of Jesus from the scriptures, "This is my body…blood"—what he is doing is declaring the bread and wine to be the body and blood of Christ. He does this not on his own initiative or because of his personal power. He does this action at God's gracious invitation and he acts "in the person of Christ" at Mass, not in his own person alone. But what is at stake here is a prayer that invokes God's almighty power. When we speak in the Mass, something happens, and that something is an act of God to transform gifts into Christ's body and blood and to change us who share in the Eucharist into more complete reflections of Christ in the world. What happens when we use the words of Christ is that bread and wine change: they become something they were not before, and they are now our nourishment for the journey to eternal life. When this transformed bread and wine are eaten and drunk, they are truly our act of communion—with God in Christ and with one another. But even if they are not consumed then and there, they remain what they have become through God's power and will. They don't revert to their former nature. They are what they have become and remain the body and blood of Christ. What the spoken words effected in the eucharistic change continues even after the Mass has ended. Or, in the words of the philosopher, "What is, is."

Now to the practice of the church. From the earliest records we have of the primitive eucharistic celebrations (second and third centuries), it is clear that the whole assembly shared in both the consecrated bread and wine. It is also equally clear that when the Mass ended, deacons were sent forth to distribute the eucharistic elements to those who were absent because of ill health, age, or other reasons. This means that the church's practice presumed that the eucharistic elements of Christ's body and blood remained precisely that after the Mass ended. The eucharistic action led to eucharistic distribution after Mass. This also led to the church reserving the eucharistic species in a safe place so that it could be taken to those near death (as *viaticum*). Logically, because the Eucharist was reserved for the Communion of the sick, this led to the practice that it was adored through acts of devotion. But again, all this developed because of the belief that what happened at Mass truly transformed bread and wine into Christ's body and blood. What was effected through God's power could not be undone.

94. Can someone receive Communion more than once in a day? Under what conditions?

The traditional discipline of the church has been that one can receive the Eucharist only once per day. This teaching was reiterated in 1973 in the Vatican document "On Facilitating Reception of Communion in Certain Circumstances" (the Latin title is *Immensae Caritatis*). However, in addition to reiterating the once-per-day norm, the document goes on to state certain circumstances when a person may receive more than once a day. In general, the instruction is that one may receive more than once at a Mass for special circumstances, and that one may not receive more than once simply for devotional reasons. One may receive more than once at a day at "ritual Masses," that is, a Mass for the celebration of a sacrament (such as baptism, confirmation, ordination); for the consecration of a church or altar; for the dead (funeral, anniversary, and so on); on the occasion of a bishop's or a major superior's visitation; during a special spiritual congress, meeting, or pilgrimage; and at a Mass when viaticum is administered to a dying person.

95. If I choose not to receive Communion during Mass, do I still fulfill my Sunday obligation?

The direct answer is yes. Sunday obligation requires that we participate in the Mass but it does not specify that one must receive Communion. However, the value of receiving Communion on a regular basis was first recalled in the modern era by Pope Pius X (in the document *Quam Singulari* in 1910), who urged frequent reception and lowered the age for first Communion to that "of reason." In addition, the church has traditionally underscored the value of receiving Communion during the Easter season. This is called "Easter Duty" (or the "Eucharistic Precept"). Because of the importance of celebrating the sacraments of initiation at the Easter Vigil, it was not surprising that the church paid special attention to celebrating the Eucharist during the whole fifty days of the Easter season. In 1215, at the Fourth Lateran Council, it was decreed that Catholics had to receive Communion at least during this season. The contemporary application of this is in the present (1983) *Code of Canon Law*, which specifies this obligation during the time from Palm Sunday of the Passion of the Lord through Pentecost. In the United States, this period has been extended from the first Sunday of Lent to Trinity Sunday (the Sunday after Pentecost).

One ecumenical note is worth mentioning. It was not uncommon for many non-Catholic Christian churches not to celebrate the

Eucharist every Sunday but instead to celebrate a Liturgy of the Word, with the sermon as a central element of the rite. What has happened in the past thirty or so years is that the Catholic insistence on the Eucharist being celebrated every Sunday has been adopted by Protestant churches, which now see great value in this traditional practice.

96. Is it ever acceptable to receive Communion at a service that isn't Roman Catholic? Isn't it "equivalent" to Catholic Communion?

Your specific question is addressed in the present *Code of Canon Law*. Because of the importance of this tersely worded norm, let me quote it in full:

> Whenever necessity requires it or true spiritual advantage suggests it, and provided that danger of error or of indifferentism is avoided, the Christian faithful for whom it is physically or morally impossible to approach a Catholic minister are permitted to receive the sacraments of penance, Eucharist, and anointing of the sick from non-Catholic ministers in whose Churches these sacraments are valid. (canon 844, § 2)

The origin of this statement is the text of the Decree on Ecumenism of the Second Vatican Council (n. 8 and 15). This norm has been repeated in two of Pope John Paul II's encyclicals, *Ut Unum Sint* (n. 46) and *Ecclesia de Eucharistia* (n. 44), thus showing its importance and contemporary relevance. First of all, this norm underscores the inherently public nature of the Eucharist by insisting that there be no question of scandalizing others by our actions because they might misunderstand either our belief in what the Eucharist is or what church we belong to. Next is the question of the impossibility of approaching a Catholic minister. This means that we would not go to Communion at a non-Catholic Christian wedding, funeral, or other occasion simply because of courtesy. If there is a Catholic church nearby, we are to attend our own church for sacraments. However, if a person is near death or in a location where there is no Catholic church or priest, while on vacation, for example, then we may approach a non-Catholic minister, provided that the last stipulation is met, namely, that these sacraments are considered valid by Roman Catholics.

This is often where the problem arises. For the sacraments to be considered valid requires that the priest who presides at the Eucharist be validly ordained in a church with apostolic succession, meaning that his ordination line can be traced back to the first apostles. Orthodox Catholic belief holds that only a validly ordained bishop or priest in the succession from the apostles to the present can preside at Mass. You see, not every church from the time of the Reformation espoused the value of the hierarchy (bishops, priests, and deacons). Rather, some insisted on a comparatively egalitarian idea of liturgical leadership and church government. We Catholics are accustomed to the hierarchy and know that the body of bishops in the church are our doctrinal and spiritual leaders. Their authority in these matters comes from the first apostles, and the tradition that they received from Christ has been handed on to succeeding generations in the church. This is not so familiar in non–Roman Catholic Christian churches. It is essentially for this reason that Catholics cannot say that the Eucharist of other churches is always the same as ours. For example, this means that we recognize the validity of the ordinations of priests in the Eastern Churches but not that of all Protestant churches, because of what they believe or don't believe about ordination.

This norm is reiterated in the 1993 *Directory for Ecumenism* (from the Pontifical Council for Promoting Christian Unity), which same document underscores our closeness with the Eastern Churches and allows that, given situations of necessity, we might approach them for sacraments. What remains unspecified, however, is precisely what *other* churches this might refer to. The concrete issue for American Catholics is what Protestant churches this might imply, now or in the future. I suspect that this is deliberately left open in this text because the Vatican is engaged in high-level discussions with a number of Christian churches (Anglicans, Lutherans, Methodists, and others) on international and national levels about matters of doctrine and practice. The church's general norms as stated in canon law and this *Directory* leave open the possibility of our drawing together on matters of faith and practice. The U.S. bishops faced this question in 1986 and again in 1996 when they issued "Guidelines for Communion Reception," which I quote in full in my answer to question 97. It is a succinct pastoral instruction for our country, drafted to meet our particular needs.

Certainly pain and personal suffering surround these issues, especially when we face the lack of unity in faith within our own families. The stance of the Catholic Church since Vatican II has been far more open and invitational than in the years preceding it. However, when the norms underscore the importance of avoiding "indifferentism," it suggests that "free and easy access" to sacraments of other Christian churches is not envisioned and is not to be fostered. Hence, when attending weddings and funerals under normal circumstances in other churches, we are to refrain from receiving Communion because we do not share the fullness of faith with them.

When I was growing up, I often heard the saying that "the family that prays together, stays together." At least partially, what the church's present legislation on Communion underscores is the concept that "the family that believes together, shares Communion together." Note that I used the terms *family* and *together*. Because we share common belief, we share a common eucharistic table.

Now, our sharing in communion is not meant to signify that we are perfect, totally united, or sinless—far from it! After all, if we were, then we wouldn't need sacraments in the first place. The issue here is whether we have a sufficient degree of belonging to one another in the church so as to share in communion to make our belief less imperfect and our common life less disunited. One of the purposes of the Mass is that we may become less and less imperfect as God's pilgrim church on earth. But it is because we go to God together in the meantime, in the church, that we share faith and sacraments with one another in the same church with people who share the same faith. The scandal of a disunited Christianity hits home especially in this sensitive issue. Our annual week of prayer for Christian unity at the end of January (18 to 25) and occasional ecumenical services of the Word stand as continual reminders that we still need to strive for that perfect unity for which Jesus prayed: "That all may be one."

97. Today, some priests invite everybody to receive Holy Communion during funerals and weddings, even non-Catholics or Catholics who do not receive sacraments regularly or attend Mass weekly. Can you explain?

I think I have answered at least part of your question in replying to the previous question. In addition I'd like to point to the "Guidelines for Reception of Communion" that the U.S. bishops drafted in 1996, which takes into consideration Catholics, "fellow Christians," and "non-Christians." They state:

For Catholics

As Catholics, we fully participate in the celebration of the Eucharist when we receive Holy Communion. We are encouraged to receive Communion devoutly and frequently. In order to be properly disposed to receive Communion, participants should not be conscious of grave sin and normally should have fasted for one hour. A person who is conscious of grave sin is not to receive the Body and Blood of the Lord without prior sacramental confession except for a grave reason where there is no opportunity for confession. In this case the person is to be mindful of the obligation to make an act of perfect contrition, including the intention of confessing as soon as possible (canon 916). A frequent reception of the Sacrament of Penance is encouraged for all.

For our fellow Christians

We welcome our fellow Christians to this celebration of the Eucharist as our brothers and sisters. We pray that our common baptism and the action of the Holy Spirit in this Eucharist will draw us closer to one another and begin to dispel the sad divisions which separate us. We pray that these will lessen and finally disappear, in keeping with Christ's prayer for us "that they may all be one" (John 17:21).

Because Catholics believe that the celebration of the Eucharist is a sign of the reality of the oneness of faith, life, and worship, members of those churches with whom we are not yet fully united are ordinarily not admitted to Holy Communion. Eucharistic sharing in exceptional circumstances by other Christians requires permission according to the directives of the diocesan bishop and the provisions of canon law (canon 844.4). Members of the Orthodox Churches, the Assyrian Church of the East, and the Polish National Catholic Church are urged to respect the discipline of their own Churches. According to Roman Catholic discipline, the Code of Canon Law does not object to the reception of Communion by Christians of these Churches (canon 844.3).

For those not receiving Holy Communion

All who are not receiving Holy Communion are encouraged to express in their hearts a prayerful desire for unity with the Lord Jesus and with one another.

For non-Christians

We also welcome to this celebration those who do not share our faith in Jesus Christ. While we cannot admit

them to Holy Communion, we ask them to offer their
prayers for the peace and unity of the human family.

When addressing Catholics specifically, these guidelines state
that one "should not be conscious of grave sin," that a person who
is conscious of grave sin "is not to receive the Body and Blood of
the Lord without prior sacramental confession," but if there is no
such opportunity, the individual has "the obligation to make an act
of perfect contrition, including the intention of confessing as soon
as possible." I think you will agree that these norms are clear and
are worded in a pastorally sensitive way. This has been taken up
again by the American bishops in their 2006 document *Happy Are
Those Who Are Called to His Supper: On Preparing to Receive Christ
Worthily in the Eucharist.*

But the pastoral reality is a bit more complex. The percentage of
American Catholics who say they are Catholic and who participate in
Sunday Mass is somewhere around one-third of those who should be
participating. This means that there are far more Catholics choosing
not to celebrate Mass than who choose to do so. Is their lack of atten-
dance a grave sin? Our tradition says that it is. In practice I suspect that
many no longer think that way. (Whether this *should* be what they
think is another matter.) So what happens at the pastorally sensitive situations of weddings and funerals is that many Catholics who do not
regularly participate at Sunday Mass choose to receive Communion.
Some priests I know try to anticipate this situation by offering to hear
confessions after a Christian wake service or after a wedding rehearsal.
On the other hand, given the severe decline of priests, it is often
enough the case that wake services and wedding rehearsals are conducted by other persons (deacons or laypersons) so that this pastoral
"solution" is not always possible. In addition, this same phenomenon
of the decline in the number of priests has itself contributed to the
decline in the frequency of sacramental penance. With fewer priests
available, fewer people avail themselves of confession.

What is clearly the intention of the American bishops in issu-
ing these guidelines is that they be printed in worship aids and

made available for catechesis, so that people are aware of church teaching and practice, especially at these pastorally sensitive occasions. There is nothing to suggest that priests should announce to the whole assembly that everyone is invited to Communion. Such a statement goes against the fundamental norm of personal conscience—one makes judgments about one's soul and life before God. That a priest would make a general announcement takes this choice away from an individual. Hopefully the published guidelines will help people come to terms with the issue of the frequency of their Mass participation and their use of the sacrament of penance.

Regarding non-Catholics, this is one of the most sensitive issues that regularly surfaces in pastoral practice. In fact, a friend of mine who conducts a weekly session for "inquirers" about the Catholic faith (a group that leads to some participants becoming catechumens and eventually baptized Catholics) repeatedly tells me that this is the most frequently asked question at those meetings and the one that causes the greatest controversy. As she says, on the one hand the church wants to be invitational about sharing the Eucharist by encouraging regular reception of Communion; but on the other hand it limits who can come to the eucharistic table.

What is going on here has a number of levels of meaning and they need careful explanation. The issue about who may receive has deep roots, is complex, and has much more to do with what we believe in general and the meaning of church belonging than the particular act of taking Communion at Mass. Let me start by noting that the Eucharist is a sacrament of initiation and, in fact, is the sacrament that ends the act of sacramental initiation for adults at Easter (water baptism, confirmation, and Eucharist). The theological principle here is that one must first be baptized (and adults must also be confirmed) before they can receive the Eucharist. The reason is that one needs to make an act of faith in the triune God, Father, Son, and Spirit, be immersed in the living waters of the baptismal font (or have water poured on them), and be anointed with the chrism of salvation with the seal of the Holy Spirit. All of this is the church's liturgical way of celebrating our new life in Christ, which is then ratified and renewed every time we celebrate the Eucharist. This means that while the church is invitational and wants all to receive new life in Christ, it also insists that we be members of Christ's body through baptism and confirmation before we share in the sacred meal of the Eucharist. As early as the thanksgiving prayer contained in the *Didache* (a treatise from around the year 100), the church stated: "Let no one eat or drink of your eucharist except those baptized in the name of the Lord. 'Do not give what is holy to dogs'" (*Didache*, n. 9, quoting Matt 7:6).

Now the questions arise: who is baptized, and what does it mean to belong to the church? Contemporary church teaching recognizes that baptisms in non–Roman Catholic Christian churches that are performed in water (immersing or pouring) and with the invocation of the Trinity (Father, Son, and Holy Spirit) are true baptisms and make one a member of the household of Christ. But does this automatically mean that anyone so baptized can share in the Eucharist? No. And here the plot thickens for an important theological reason: belief in orthodox Catholic teaching about the Eucharist. The principal reason why not everyone whose baptism is recognized as valid can share in our Eucharist has to do with the church's teachings about the Eucharist itself. To receive Communion at a Catholic Eucharist means that the person affirms all that the Catholic Church teaches about the Eucharist—most specifically, that it is the real presence and that it is a sacrifice. So for non-Catholics to think about coming to share in our Eucharist, they first must believe what the church teaches about the real presence of Christ in the sacrament. Concretely, what this leads to is a situation in which not all the baptized share in the same set of beliefs, and this is what causes us not to invite members of other Christian churches to the Eucharist, under normal conditions.

Put as simply as I can: normally we share communion with others in the same church who profess the same beliefs (particularly about the Eucharist and ordination). In cases of true necessity, certain conditions must be met, including at least substantial unity in belief. We should never seek to proselytize or change another's belief; we may, however, invite them to understand Roman Catholic beliefs and practices. What I see as the real difficulty here is that we don't often appreciate the relationship between sharing eucharistic Communion on the one hand and sharing our beliefs and our belonging to the church on the other. These are of a piece, and we should strive to deepen that awareness that you can't have one without the other.

This brings me to another distinction that has to do with unity in belief systems. From the time of the Crusades (the eleventh century), preexisting tensions between Eastern and Western Christians reached the breaking point so that while today there is a substantial ground of common teaching and belief, there is a clear separation between us. The causes for this separation stem from both sides. Some of the issues concern the way we describe who Christ is, and some concern the authority of the pope and Rome in relation to other church leaders ("patriarchs"). Certainly the contemporary East-West dialogues about the theology of the church and sacraments have helped move us toward more complete unity. But we are not there yet!

X

The Eucharist and Daily Life

98. I used to love the Tridentine Mass, when the Mass seemed like a special time between God and me. Now with all the emphasis on participation I feel that it is a less sacred and holy time. Can you help me?

In responding to the questions in part three on the "Reform of the Liturgy" (as well as in other places), I have tried to offer the explanation of why the Mass has changed by using church documents and the Missal itself. Your question hits at some of these issues, so I'd ask you to refer back to those responses. But what I'd like to do here is to frame an answer that deals with your phrase about the Mass as a "sacred and holy time." Certainly the prescribed rituals of the extraordinary form of the Mass can foster a sense of otherness, splendor, and pageantry. The formality of the Mass, the colors and design of the vestments, regular use of incense at high and solemn Masses, Latin chant music—all play a part in fostering our appreciation of the Mass as something out of the ordinary and otherworldly, a spectacle that affords us an opportunity to experience the Eucharist as a miracle that depends on God's overarching and sustaining grace. While we know we are unworthy of this gift, the Tridentine Mass certainly underscores the distance and separation between us humans and God's infinite holiness. But at the same time, much of what this ritual "accomplishes" in these ways can also be accomplished in the *Novus Ordo Missae* in Latin. Notice I said "much," because the *Novus Ordo Missae* does expect a greater sense of participation than the extraordinary form of the Mass.

There were some elements of the Tridentine Mass that the highest church authority and the best of liturgical scholars argued should be changed. In addressing the primary goal of the reform, the bishops at Vatican II repeatedly cited "full, conscious and active participation" as a chief goal of the changes in the liturgy ushered in with the council. Now in the implementation of the reformed liturgy, I suspect that a great deal happened that upset people and caused a disturbance in their experience of the utter transcendence and otherness of God that they had come to experience in the Tridentine Mass. But to be honest, I have to say that some of this may not have been bad. As Christians we believe in many paradoxes, not the least of which is God's total otherness and yet, through Christ especially, God's immediate closeness to us, as one of us in his human nature. The Mass is supposed to reflect both the transcendence and immanence of God. If, in fact, the Tridentine Rite emphasized God's transcendence, one of the legitimate criticisms made against it was that it was so otherworldly that it was not a vehicle for adequate participation, comprehension, and appropriation into daily life.

So I would argue that Vatican II's purpose of revising the liturgy was well served in order to emphasize God's closeness to us and to allow us, especially through the vernacular, to comprehend the prayers and readings and seek to fulfill them by what we say and do both during the Mass and in daily life itself. In a sense, then, based on the kind of God we believe in and pray to at Mass, it is not really appropriate to look to the Mass—whether in the extraordinary or the ordinary form—as a "sacred and holy time" that is removed from daily life. It is better to see the rites and prayers, sounds and rhythms of the liturgy as a special, unique, and especially powerful experience of God, transcendent and immanent, but an experience that also draws us into deeper contact with God in all of life.

For me, a useful way to describe what the Mass is meant to be comes from the event of the Transfiguration. The disciples ascend a high mountain, experience the word of revelation, and see the transfigured Christ, only to leave the mountain and descend back to daily life, sustained and uplifted by that experience. The disciples did not remain on the mountain forever. Nor should we view the act of liturgy as the only place we discover God's sacredness and holiness. We do indeed experience it at Mass, in both its forms, but we also are then encouraged to discover God in daily life as well—and whenever we discover God, it is a "sacred and holy" thing.

Parts of the Mass foster this interrelationship: for example, the General Intercessions and the Sign of Peace. In fact, the intercessions were not a part of the Tridentine Mass, and when the Sign of Peace was exchanged in the former rite, it was among the ministers in the sanctuary only. These parts have been restored and can now become important vehicles for the linking of liturgy with life, connecting our experience of God at Mass with the expression of God's mercy and love toward one another. Although many saw the reintroduction of the Sign of Peace as a severe interruption in the solemnity of the Mass, its meaning (as described by St. Augustine and countless others; see question 72) was to ratify who we are and what we are about at Mass and in life.

99. How does celebrating Mass on Sunday relate to or connect with daily Christian life all during the week?

I hinted at part of this in replying to the previous question. Your question allows me to deepen what I said there and to add to it. I think it was the composer Jerome Kern who wrote the song "Two Different Worlds We Live In." I don't want to disparage this piece of music or the sentiment of the song. But I do want to take issue with this as a way of looking at the Christian life or as a way of describing how the "sacred" and the "secular" are separable and separated parts of the Christian life.

In fact, we live in *one* world, a world that God loved so much that he sent his Son into it to save us by becoming one of us. So we should view the Mass not as a refuge from life. Rather, we should see it as a matrix, as a place where the concerns of daily life intersect with God's transcendence and immanence. The whole dynamic of gathering for Mass is that we come together in order to go our separate ways when it has ended. In preparing for Mass,

I'd suggest that before coming together to participate, we pray over
the scriptures that will be proclaimed and reflect on the events of
our lives and the lives of those we love. This kind of reflective
prayer is crucial in order that what the liturgy presumes to happen
will happen: that what we pray be reflective of what we believe and
what we live outside of the liturgy. To amplify the traditional phrase
"the law of prayer establishes the law of belief," I'd like to say that
what we pray and what we celebrate together should have a direct
impact on how we evaluate life and conduct our daily lives.

Among the many places where the Mass articulates this belief
are the following: in the General Intercessions, in the Presentation of
the Gifts, when eucharistic ministers (and deacons) take Communion from the Mass to those who cannot attend, and at the Dismissal
at the end of Mass. In the General Intercessions, the needs of the
community are summarized in prayer. We offer our own needs and
we are stretched to include the needs of others. What we bring forward as gifts for the Mass—bread, wine, monetary gifts—should
reflect our daily lives and our very selves. We present bread and wine,
the product of human manufacture, and these gifts become the
means for our sharing in the body and blood of Christ. They also
reflect human work—what we do outside in human labor has a deep
bearing on what we bring to Mass. (In the words of the late Cardinal
Basil Hume: "No work, no Mass.") When ministers bring the
Eucharist to the homebound, we send them with our prayers. The
prayers the ministers use on these occasions reflect and recall our
prayers at Mass for those who could not be with us. Finally, the
Dismissal Rite itself is designed to make these connections. Any
announcements at the end of Mass are to make the connection
between liturgy and daily parish concerns. And the Dismissal texts
themselves summarize succinctly much of what the Mass is about—
"Go forth, the Mass is ended," "Go and announce the Gospel of the
Lord," and "Go in peace, glorifying the Lord by your life"—living
what we have shared through God's grace and love.

Another significant example of this intrinsic link between
liturgy and daily life and a reminder that we live in *one* graced

world is the restoration of the diaconate as a permanent liturgical ministry. In all the revised rites since Vatican II, the role of the deacon is presumed as a constitutive part of every liturgical rite. The restoration of this ministry is not just for the sake of the liturgy— it is also for the sake of diaconal service outside of the liturgy. As I have argued before, the deacon was the central minister who bridged worship and social ministry. It was the deacon who served at the Lord's altar table because he served the hungry from foodstuffs collected at Mass. It was the deacon who proclaimed the gospel, and it was the deacon who preached the gospel by words and, more poignantly, by the kind of passion he lived for spreading God's justice in the world. It was the deacon who proclaimed the intercessions, because through his ministry in the community, it was he who would know who was sick or in special need. The restoration of this ministry in the church is especially significant because he acts as Christ the Servant at the table of the Lord at Mass and at the table of those most in need, the poor. Therefore, there is much at stake when deacons function liturgically and minister in the life of the church. They personify and exemplify that we live in one graced world, not in "two different worlds."

100. I've heard the phrase *liturgical spirituality* but don't know what it means. Does it refer to the Mass in any way?

There are several ways to approach your very crucial question—I say *crucial* because unless we deepen our appreciation of liturgy as derived from and leading to a richer spiritual life, we may well be guilty of fostering an empty ritualism—which is certainly the furthest thing from the kind of liturgical reform that Vatican II invited. One of the main themes of the pioneers who worked toward the renewal of the liturgy in this century was that the liturgy needed to be restored as the prayer and work of the people. In fact, it was Pius X who argued that the reform of the liturgy was crucial for serving the renewal of the church—in order, as his motto said, "to restore all things in Christ." One part of this needed reform concerned the revision of devotions. The Liturgy Constitution (n. 13) urges that popular devotions be revised so that they are in accord with the sacred liturgy and the liturgical seasons. This means, for example, that the balance of praise and petition that the liturgy preserves be observed in popular devotions as well. It also implies that the liturgy, as the church's official prayer, has a certain qualitative priority over other acts of devotion. Therefore, the liturgy was not the only thing that needed reform, and when it was reformed, the church's rites clearly were to influence other kinds of prayer and piety. (This is dealt with in an extensive way in the important document entitled *Directory on Popular Piety and the Liturgy*, published by the Congregation for Divine Worship in 2001.)

The Liturgy Constitution also states that the spiritual life "is not limited solely to participation in the liturgy" (n. 12), but that other kinds of prayer are required for Christians. I like to illustrate this relationship of the liturgy (as central and pivotal) to other acts of prayer and devotion and to living the spiritual life itself by using three concentric circles (similar to the target for the game of darts or the bull's-eye in archery). In this illustration the central circle is *liturgy*. It is in the center because, according to the Liturgy Constitution, it is "the summit toward which the activity of the Church is directed; at the same time it is the font from which the Church's power flows" (n. 10). After all, the liturgy comprises the rites, prayers, and ceremonies that are held in common by the whole church throughout the world. The liturgy also comprises all the aspects of our lives before God, from sacramental initiation through rites of dying and death. Also, the liturgy includes the daily celebration of the Liturgy of the Hours as well as occasional services such as religious profession. It is the key, the hinge, the central focus of all of the spiritual life.

But clearly the spiritual life is larger than taking part in rites—it involves *life* itself. So for me, the next of the circles would be labeled *prayer*. The fact that it is a circle that surrounds *liturgy* is one way of illustrating that indeed the liturgy itself is always a prayer. But the fact that this circle is wider than liturgy is meant to indicate that Christians are to engage in other acts of prayer and devotion—not just the liturgy. And when we look (proudly) at our Catholic tradition, I think we can justifiably say that the many schools of prayer (monastic, mendicant, apostolic, and so on) all reflect the Catholic genius of emphasizing that prayer is crucial while providing a number of ways to express that value.

The final, largest, and widest circle is labeled *spirituality*. This is the largest because for me the living of the Christian life as converted and committed people is the chief aim of all our prayer, devotions, and pious exercises, including the liturgy. The aim of the liturgy in this sense is to reflect what we celebrate in living the spiritual life with one another before and in the world. This draws out what I have already hinted at—namely, that the real purpose of reforming the rites of the Mass is to help us appreciate what we celebrate in it and to help us live what we celebrate in our daily lives. It is crucial to underscore that at Mass the bread and wine become the body and blood of Christ so that we who share in these gifts at Communion can be the more adequate representatives and reflection of Christ before the world as members of the Body of Christ. There is always the challenge dimension of every act of liturgy. We are always directed to live what we celebrate, to reflect what we celebrate ritually in the way we relate to each other and witness to God's love in the world.

Spirituality is also the largest of the circles and "contains" prayer and liturgy in that spirituality depends on prayer and liturgy for it to be authentic, Christian, theological, and other-directed. This is critical, I would argue, especially today, because of a lot that passes as "contemporary spirituality." The delusion may well be that New Age crystals, the seemingly omnipresent representations of angels, and the plethora of self-help and advice books on the bestseller lists today may well be self-delusional. I say this because Catholic spirituality always requires a liturgical prayer component, and always implies an other-directed, self-sacrificing, and service component. Catholic spirituality needs liturgy as its mainstay and anchor; it requires that we pray communally and privately to God through Christ in the power of the Holy Spirit in intercession for and with the wider church. And Catholic spirituality in its best stripe always requires that we love and serve others, not just those of our intimate circle in family and friends, or those with whom we agree. Catholic spirituality demands that we imitate Jesus in washing one another's feet, in helping to carry others' crosses, and in sharing others' burdens.

In an era that prizes the *self*, this is certainly nothing short of a clear, countercultural challenge. But to be true to our faith and to our tradition's understanding of liturgy, prayer, and spirituality, we can and may do no other. In a sense this makes liturgy—true liturgy, not just rubrics and rites—nothing short of subversive of the status quo and very challenging of the way things are. But then again, Jesus' dining habits in the gospels were equally subversive and challenging. Therefore, we can do and be no other.

101. I hear a lot these days about linking the Eucharist and issues of justice. Can you help me understand why these are to be so interrelated?

Your question is very contemporary and yet recalls a very traditional theme of our faith and of our liturgy. It is not surprising to note how issues of justice and the liturgy are related, given the fact that at Vatican II and thereafter issues of global justice and peace occupied the bishops at the council and in the subsequent synod on "Justice in the World," and given the fact that after Vatican II, Pope Paul VI established an institutional form for this concern by founding the Pontifical Council on Justice and Peace at the Vatican. That liturgy and justice should be so linked today is a notable and significant revival of part of what I argued in response to the previous question, namely, that liturgy always has implications for human life and that our participation in liturgy should lead to ever deeper participation in living holy and just lives before God in service to others.

Among the notable aspects of reuniting liturgy and justice is that the very notion of *justice* requires that we leave behind any domestic, overly intimate, or familial notions of what liturgy is all about. When we use the term *justice*, we are immediately directed toward the whole gamut of the way the world limits true justice, particularly in terms of class divisions, tribal conflicts, color or gender discrimination, and so on. When all of that is in the forefront of our celebration of liturgy, then the widest lens possible is put on what liturgy should focus on—concerns that are nothing short of global.

At the same time, when we speak of liturgy and justice we are immediately concerned with the fact that what we celebrate is the challenge and gift of *God's* justice. This means that any notions of what justice is derive from the gospels, and these often overturn human expectations in favor of what God has in store for us. This means laying ourselves open to the challenge of a paradoxical parable in which the same wage is given to all who work in the vineyard, no matter the number of hours (Matt 20:1–16), or the parable of the prodigal son (Luke 15). In each of these, human logic and our native sense of distributive "justice" is overturned in favor of the overwhelming kindness and amazing grace of God. It is this kind of justice that should be the measure of the world's and the church's expectations, but so often it is not. All too often we fall back into something akin to what is really condemned in the gospels—an eye for an eye and a tooth for a tooth—whereas God's justice measures out mercy, not condemnation; grace, not judgment.

In this sense it is most helpful that justice and liturgy have been reunited. Hopefully this will mean that God's often confounding, always liberating power will break through these rites and ceremonies so that what we experience is an ever more complete identification with God through Christ. It is, after all, he whom we invoke during Advent when we cry, "Let the clouds rain down the Just One." And it is his paschal dying and rising that we take part in ("participate in") each time we celebrate the Mass, from which we are sent forth, as two of the prayers for Dismissal put it, to

"Go and announce the Gospel of the Lord…

"Go in peace, glorifying the Lord by your life."

Other Books
Under the Former Series Title